Zimbabwe since the Unity Government

Zimbabwe has moved from a condition of restricted expression to one of many contradictory expressions. Politics has lost none of its compromises and conflicts, but it has been amplified by an explosion of voices. For the first time, a genuine debate is possible among many actors, insiders and outsiders, and the question marks over Zimbabwe and its future are no longer in terms of a narrow choice between one party and another, one outlook or another. Compromise government has meant complexity of debate. This does not preclude disillusionment within debate, but it does include vigour and imagination in debate.

This book includes essays from renowned scholars, governmental and diplomatic figures, and prioritises contributions by Zimbabweans themselves. The essays provide a blend of academic and practitioner observation and judgement which no other volume has done.

This book was first published as a special issue of *The Round Table*.

Stephen Chan was a member of the 1980 Commonwealth Observer Group that oversaw the independence of Zimbabwe. He was Foundation Dean at SOAS, where he remains Professor of International Relations. He has published the authoritative works on both Robert Mugabe and Morgan Tsvangirai.

Ranka Primorac is Lecturer in English at Southampton. She lived for nine years in Zimbabwe and has published several books on the literature of the country, including the authoritative *The Place of Tears*, (2006). Together, they edited the Routledge book, *Zimbabwe in Crisis*, (2007).

Zimbabwe since the Unity Government

Edited by
Stephen Chan and Ranka Primorac

Routledge
Taylor & Francis Group

LONDON AND NEW YORK

First published 2013
by Routledge
2 Park Square, Milton Park, Abingdon, Oxon, OX14 4RN

Simultaneously published in the USA and Canada
by Routledge
711 Third Avenue, New York, NY 10017

Routledge is an imprint of the Taylor & Francis Group, an informa business

British Library Cataloguing in Publication Data
A catalogue record for this book is available from the British Library

ISBN13: 978-0-415-62484-8

Typeset in Times New Roman
by Taylor & Francis Books

Publisher's Note
The publisher would like to make readers aware that the chapters in this book may be referred to as articles as they are identical to the articles published in the special issue. The publisher accepts responsibility for any inconsistencies that may have arisen in the course of preparing this volume for print.

Printed and bound in Great Britain by
TJ International Ltd, Padstow, Cornwall

Contents

Citation Information

The following chapters were originally published in *The Round Table*, volume 99, issue 411 (December 2010). When citing this material, please use the original page numbering for each article, as follows:

Introduction: Zimbabwe since the Unity Government - The Space of Many Voices

Stephen Chan and Ranka Primorac

When we edited issue 411 of *The Round Table* in December 2010, it followed upon our book, *Zimbabwe in Crisis* (Primorac and Chan, 2007), which described a Zimbabwe in which the power-sharing government had not yet come into existence. An entire range of key issues and/or voices in the national debate seemed suppressed or stifled – and the articles we gathered together sought to demonstrate this. Since the advent of the power-sharing government, marked by the swearing-in of Prime Minister Morgan Tsvangirai on 11 February 2009, almost all public commentary has been to the effect that Zimbabwe's new government is a coalition of unequal parts, and that both groupings of the former opposition Movement for Democratic Change (MDC) were either ineffectual, or being persistently and successfully bludgeoned into a junior role. The purpose of this book, based upon the special issue of *The Round Table*, is not to dispute, but to refine and problematise this simple picture. Notwithstanding the many political machinations, stalemates and bad faith, debate and plurality of expression have increased in Zimbabwe. The special issue was released at the end of 2010 and much has happened since then. In particular, elections loom and, at time of writing, there is no certainty as to when they will be. They could be as early as Autumn 2012, as this book is being released, or as late as Easter to June 2013. Both the MDC and the regional grouping, SADC (the Southern African Development Community), would prefer the 2013 date – but Robert Mugabe's ZANU-PF party has within it many zealots who would like to push for a 2012 poll. They reason they would still benefit from Mugabe's leadership – he would be much frailer in 2013, should he live that long – and they could bully if not bludgeon their way to power yet again. But much has changed, not only within the political parties, but within the electorate. A corrupt and violent election would be harder to hold. Even with a living Mugabe, it would be harder than in the elections of 2008. As it is, Mugabe's health has been the subject of ever more frenzied speculation, especially whenever he visits Singapore (where he does indeed receive medical assistance); and, with the greater difficulties in using large measures of violence, ZANU-PF has worked towards a platform of indigenisation – following the nationalisation of farms with that of 51% of companies. But it must still subject itself to a plural vocality.

The multiplicity of voices is due in part to the fractionation of almost all the key players in Zimbabwean politics. Robert Mugabe's ZANU-PF suffered a key defection before the controversial 2008 elections, with the departure and independent Presidential candidacy of Simba Makoni (backed, it was thought, by military heavyweights such as Solomon Mujuru). As early as 2010, there were clear cleavages between military (or 'Securotocratic') ZANU-PF and civilian ZANU-PF, with further cleavages within the military as well as the civilian wings. In some ways, the party has become a loose coalescence of competitive oligarchies that benefit from 'ZANU-PF' as a name. The MDC itself split in 2006, and both the Tsvangirai and Mutambara versions of the party have since had their own dissensions. Welshman Ncube challenged Arthur Mutambara successfully for leadership of what had been the Mutambara faction – although Mutambara remains Deputy Prime Minister, albeit without a party of his own. Dumiso Dabengwa revived Joshua Nkomo's Ndebele-based ZAPU, having first himself left ZANU-PF. The Tsvangirai-led MDC's first year in office saw grave tensions between Prime Minister Morgan Tsvangirai and his Finance Minister, Tendai Biti. Those have considerably softened now and there is also the spectacle of some cross-party commonality. Biti seems to have out-manoeuvred the avaricious Central Bank Governor, ZANU-PF's Gideon Gono, who has himself been warning against excessive and ill-thought-out ZANU-PF fiscal policies. No one can fully predict how many song-lines will eventually emerge from Zimbabwe, or who will end up in whose chorus, and when.

The voices at the high levels of politics should not detract from the debates voiced across a range of Zimbabwean communities, both at home and abroad. The diaspora has, of course, long had its own multiplicity of voices, articulating both its political standpoints and its modes of self-organisation and self-help far from home. Inside Zimbabwe, unity government has also meant an increased (though still fraught) sense of being able to speak publicly in 'high-density' areas or townships (former colonial ghettos) where political thuggery has long been rife. And an MDC voice, however conditional, in government has further meant that those who were once able to act with open and mindless violence must now, at least in part, nuance their own ways of speaking.

When it is not dealing with the Western world, however, Zimbabwean foreign policy has retained a remarkable coherence with what it was before the power-sharing deal.

Yet none of this detracts from a public sphere marked by increasingly complex perfidities and despairs. An up-and-coming Zimbabwean writer (whose work is discussed in some detail in the post-script to this issue) captures the mood of the moment when, in a novel published since the unity government, he describes the oppressive, paradox-ridden atmosphere permeating a Harare township with the words: 'I felt an atmosphere of friendliness, violence, innovation, poverty, joy but one thing that hung over everything else was despair; an air of hopelessness as if everyone was in a pit that they could not climb out of.' (Huchu 2010: 26) Zimbabwe is very far from 'settling down', and probably can't until after elections deemed as free and fair. The multiplicity of public voices articulates the multiplicities of tensions, of searches for ways forwards, and frustrations that no progress ever seems to blossom, let alone bear lasting fruit. The compromises the MDC has had to make, the complete lack of selflessness among the 'hard men' of ZANU-PF, the treachery of those who ferry services back and forth – searching for opportunisms – the hardship of life within a stabilising financial regime marked only by a continuing shortage of finance, and the reposing of too much hope in recently-discovered and controversially-exploited diamond fields means that there is no repair to years of plunder and deterioration. All this marks something that we would be derelict not to point out: that the space of many voices is also a space not only of heroic voices but of sordid ones. The articles collected in this book indicate all these points and more.

It is important to stress that all full-length contributions to this issue have been written from a standpoint of closeness to material events: we have included *only* authors who are themselves resident in Zimbabwe or Southern Africa, who write with Zimbabweans and privilege interviews with Zimbabweans, or who were witnesses to events in Zimbabwe as they unfolded. No contribution has been written 'at distance'. Several of the authors have been directly politically and diplomatically involved in the events which they describe and analyse. There is therefore a mix of practitioner and academic work in this volume – but all contributions cohere around the themes high-lighted in this Introduction. Sydney Mufamadi was Mandela's youngest minister and went onto become Mbeki's key negotiator with the Zimbabwean parties both before and after the last elections. Fay King Chung was a ZANU-PF minister in the late 1980s, but stood as a Senatorial candidate backing Simba Makoni in the last elections. Brian Raftopoulos is one of the most significant civic and scholarly figures on the Zimbabwean scene.

In his contribution, Mufamadi describes how the Zimbabwean mediation fits in the triptych of negotiations which he and Thabo Mbeki crafted.[1] In Democratic Republic of Congo, Zimbabwe and Sudan, the emphasis has been on a new African 'paradigm' of inclusiveness, where the multiplicity of voices can be given common and, to an extent, unified space. Zimbabwe was not a 'one-off', as Kofi Annan's own mediation in Kenya also suggests.

Martin Welz was present in Zimbabwe for the inauguration of Prime Minister Tsvangirai and he describes the first 100 days of the unity government. He notes acutely, from the very beginning, the divisions in the parties. In an extended and important account on foreign policy under the unity government, Sabelo J. Ndlovu-Gatsheni details how the MDC has eroded ZANU-PF hegemony in terms of the framing conditions of relationships with Angola without in fact advancing a new policy.

Fay Chung charts the ZANU-PF electoral decline, and analyses the key players across the divides. She critiques Tsvangirai but sees Simba Makoni as indicative of a new pluralism that includes "the better aspects of ZANU-PF". Although the Makoni star has waned since Chung wrote for the 2010 special issue, the idea of "better aspects" within ZANU-PF is a key element in such hopefulness as may be occasionally seen in Zimbabwean politics. Both Welz and Chung write about Solomon and Joice Mujuru and, in 2012, Solomon Mujuru died in what many viewed as an assassination. He features in a multi-faceted way in the conclusion to this book.

Jocelyn Alexander and Kudakwashe Chitofiri take up the theme of the disillusionment and extend it to both MDC and ZANU-PF. Based on extensive interviews in Norton, an outlying town of Harare, they set out the brutal maltreatment MDC youth activists suffered at the hands of ZANU-PF party thugs, and how these activists now feel let down by their own party. But ZANU-PF youth activists also feel let down and betrayed. Their ability to dominate all around them has greatly narrowed and both sides feel abandoned, in their intimate neighbourhood, by the unity government. Theirs are voices that no longer can be easily categorised under the main political party labels.

Similarly, as JoAnn McGregor and Dominic Pasura discuss, new configurations have grown within Zimbabwe's diaspora, including in particular the evolving search for a non-partisan space within which development 'back home' could be assisted. The diaspora has its own tensions, but these again should not be seen in only ZANU-PF and MDC terms. In the UK, those with and those without asylum rights transact their approaches to Zimbabwe with highly peculiar tensions.

Finally, Brian Raftopoulos analyses the first two years of the unity government itself. All actors in this government have been shaped by what he calls a 'passive revolution' in which Zimbabwe has been politicised to the extent that the discourse of individuality and rights favoured by international NGOs and pressure groups is often distant from the growing realities on the ground. Raftopoulos paints a bleak picture of the political configurations and the political figures involved. This bleakness might be expressed with even more complexity, and certainly nuance, in 2012, but bleakness is a central emotional theme in how Zimbabwean polities see the prospects of clean change and clean politicians. To round the book off, but taking a different approach to that of Sydney Mufamadi, Raftopoulos looks at Mbeki's impulses behind his mediation in Zimbabwe. But the complexity and conditionalities of Raftopoulos's analysis are such that, even as we speak of many voices, we must also say that the autonomy, free agency, and range of options for any of these voices to take the country forward decisively are greatly constrained.

Notes

1 This paper was commissioned in 2010 by the Brenthurst Foundation but has never been presented or published. The Foundation graciously made it available to *The Round Table* and the Editors thank the Foundation.

References

Huchu, T. (2010) *The Hairdresser of Harare* (Auckland Park: Jacana).
Primorac, R and S. Chan, eds. (2007), Zimbabwe in Crisis: The International Response and the Space of Silence (London: Routledge).

Zimbabwe's 'Inclusive Government': Some Observations on its First 100 Days

MARTIN WELZ

University of Konstanz, Konstanz, Germany

ABSTRACT   *Zimbabwe seemed to be in a political transition—but only on the surface. In actual fact, the new government established under the power-sharing agreement between President Mugabe and newly elected Prime Minister Morgan Tsvangirai proved unsuccessful in its first 100 days owing to continued rivalry and a lack of commitment on behalf of Mugabe and his party. Mugabe managed to secure key positions in the new government for his cronies. They continued to control the relevant security organs as well as the Reserve Bank, which held a key position because its Governor guarded the budget available for the new ministers. Consequently, sabotage was an imminent threat for the new government. Mugabe benefited from the weakness of the opposition, which was split and had an indecisive and uncharismatic leader who failed to secure financial support from the West. To complicate the situation even further there were more players involved in the political arena of Zimbabwe, including the two major farmers' groupings, an emerging third party under Simba Makoni, the trade unions and white businessmen. They all had their own agenda. Mugabe and his ruling clique relied on each other as they had both committed gross human rights violations over the last 25 years. They either fall together or their mutual dependency keeps them going. Change was unlikely to occur; even the new Movement for Democratic Change ministers were aware of this.*

Introduction

Zimbabwe's new government faced severe difficulties during its first 100 days in office. The situation in Zimbabwe is very complex and the problems are deep-rooted, aggravated by many different players involved in the political arena. It remains unclear who eventually led the country in the period under scrutiny. It is assumed that there was a mutual relationship between Mugabe and the ruling clique, comprised of the heads of state security organs, the Reserve Bank Governor and other close allies of President Mugabe. They still needed each other to stay in power and to be safe from prosecution. Hence, they took the necessary steps to continue ruling the country even under the new political circumstances following the power-sharing agreement with the Movement for Democratic Change (MDC). The Zimbabwe African National Union–Patriotic Front (ZANU-PF), Mugabe's party, continued to control the realm of state security and the financial resources available to the new Prime Minister, Morgan Tsvangirai, and his cabinet, meaning that sabotage of the new government's policy was an imminent threat.

The situation during the first 100 days into the new government can be summed up by saying that Mugabe could only win, while Tsvangirai could only lose. Mugabe secured a non-interventionist stance from the states in the region, most notably South Africa. On a global level, China and Russia backed him in the United Nations Security Council. Furthermore, he benefited from the weakness of the opposition, which was split and whose leaders were weak and uncharismatic. Tsvangirai was described as being indecisive (*Africa Research Bulletin*, 2007, p. 17145A) and not assertive enough in the negotiations. The power-sharing agreement and the distribution of cabinet posts reflect this. Tsvangirai took a submissive role to Mugabe's position and entered a government that was still largely controlled by ZANU-PF. Tsvangirai had already lost politically particularly considering that he had raised high expectations and promised a great deal. In this context, he has achieved little in the first 100 days of the Inclusive Government.

This paper focuses on the first weeks after the new government was sworn in. It first reflects on my experiences in Zimbabwe in February 2009. Therefore, the first part is subjective and not explicitly rooted in academic knowledge. The second part is different in that it provides an account of the situation in Zimbabwe from early to mid-2009 on the basis of interview data, thorough newspaper reading and academic analysis. The following themes are elaborated: the first section of the second part tries to find out who effectively ruled Zimbabwe in the period under investigation. The second section scrutinises the weakness of the main opposition, namely Tsvangirai's MDC. This is followed by a section about the various domestic players involved in Zimbabwe's politics, specifically Simba Makoni's group, the farmers and the businessmen who contributed to the complexity of the political arena. The arguments made in this article refer explicitly to the first 100 days of the new government; arguably, however, to a large extent they also apply to the current situation in Zimbabwe.

Living in Zimbabwe: Some Observations

Daily life in Zimbabwe seemed unaffected by the new government after it was inaugurated in early February 2009. The prevailing atmosphere is best described by the words 'cautious optimism'. An MDC cabinet member said: 'I am cautiously optimistic, but I'm under no illusions that we have a massive challenge and huge problems that lie ahead'. Indeed, people were not euphoric and only a few thought that Zimbabwe would immediately enter into a new era.

The inauguration of the new government did not alter the precarious socio-economic situation of the country. The US dollar and the South African rand replaced Zimbabwe's hyperinflational currency, with its 13 zeros making most goods unaffordable for the masses. Although shops were stocked in the city centre of Harare, it seemed that most of the people were still relying on a subsistence economy, as they had no access to foreign currencies with which to buy food and other essentials. There were reports that there was no food security in the rural areas. Moreover, cholera kept ordinary citizens on tenterhooks. Farms were still being seized and the perceived security threat from the seemingly omnipresent Central Intelligence Organisation (CIO) agents continued as before. There were no students at the University of Zimbabwe as they had been beaten by police forces on campus a couple of days earlier, forcing university officials to adjourn all classes. Likewise, schools remained closed because teachers demanded to be paid in foreign currency.

The situation in Hatcliffe, a poor northern suburb of Harare, could be seen as representative of the country. Hatcliffe is one of the high-density areas of Zimbabwe. The people who live there are poor and mostly unemployed living in shacks. Many of them have suffered as a result of Operation Murambatsvina, the notorious operation orchestrated by ZANU-PF after the 2005 elections to 'clean' informal settlements.[1] *De facto*, the operation was conducted to punish MDC voters. After speaking to MDC supporters in Hatcliffe, it became clear that people were happy about the chain of events that led to Tsvangirai's inauguration. They were indeed hopeful. Yet at the same time they were realistic, knowing that change would not happen overnight. They were traumatised and continued to live under constant threat because Mugabe supporters were still around and were still intimidating MDC supporters. It seemed that public life was frozen in a state between hope and despair.

Months before, while the MDC was campaigning for the 2008 election, its supporters wore MDC T-shirts, inevitably meaning that the ZANU-PF thugs were able to recognise their targets. Aware of this, people were fearful of Mugabe's thugs and the CIO, who were a constant threat as its agents were infiltrating public life.

The people were fearful of an outbreak of violence. Mugabe's 85th birthday was awaited with bated breath; on that day—21 February, one week after Tsvangirai's inauguration—the streets of Harare were empty. Security around hotels was increased. The ZANU-PF youth had announced that their birthday gift for Mugabe would be to oust all white farmers in the country. MDC supporters felt additionally imperilled. Hence, caution prevailed; most people stayed at home. Yet, no major incident was reported.

Although daily life slowed down on Zimbabwe's streets, the new administration was busy. New members of the government in particular (mainly from the MDC) were running from one meeting to the next. Like MDC officials and cabinet ministers, the international diplomatic corps was almost inaccessible as they convened meeting after meeting to assess the political situation and to find strategies to cope with the changed circumstances. MDC officials claimed that they were faced with a lack of loyalty from civil servants in their ministries which contributed further to the chaotic situation in political circles. It seemed that MDC officials were surprised that they eventually joined the new administration, meaning that their long-standing hopes finally became a reality. However, whether they were really starting to determine Zimbabwe's policy will be discussed in the following section.

The Rulers of Zimbabwe

Two incidents had provided a clear indication of who was actually going to rule the country in the months to come. The South African *Mail & Guardian* (13–19 February 2009, p. 28) reported: 'Approaching Mugabe to be sworn in, Tsvangirai prematurely raised his hand, and Mugabe, in Shona, said: "No, I go first", before reading him the oath'. Second, the rhetoric used is revealing. A Western diplomat noted that President Mugabe does not use the phrase 'Unity Government' as Tsvangirai does, but 'Inclusive Government'. In fact, Mugabe and his ZANU-PF were not willing to be left in the shadow. Mugabe claimed one month after the new government came into existence: 'I am still in control and hold executive power' (*The Economist*, 7 March 2009, p. 57). Tsvangirai seemed to understand that he was second behind Mugabe. He did not become as influential as he would have liked. In an interview with the South African-based *Business Day* (29 May 2009) after 100 days in office, he had already adopted Mugabe's language and also used the phrase 'Inclusive Government'.

However, it would be naïve to assume that it was only Mugabe who ruled the country before the inauguration of the Inclusive Government and during the period thereafter, which is primarily scrutinised in this paper. Many different theories are aired about who was—and arguably in 2010 still is—ruling Zimbabwe. They range from 'Mugabe is ruling the country on his own' to 'Mugabe is the puppet of the ruling clique'. Others emphasise the importance of the First Lady Grace Mugabe, while another group subscribes to the theory that the Attorney General's role is crucial. A last group emphasises the pivotal role of Reserve Bank Governor Gideon Gono. Remarkably there was no one at this stage who assumed that the new Inclusive Government had taken over power.

Each of the theories listed above bears some truth. It is argued here that the most logical way of explaining the political situation prevailing in Zimbabwe is to understand it as a mutual dependency between the ruling clique and President Mugabe that influences their behaviour towards the MDC and other players. This dependency was founded as a result of the gross human rights violations against Zimbabwe's own population, which were carried out following instructions allegedly given by the President and his closest allies. The most prominent examples of atrocities committed in the last 25 years are the 'ethnic genocide' (Gevisser, 2008, p. 297) in Matabeleland in the 1980s and Operation Murambatsvina after the election of 2005, when opposition voters were brutally beaten and—in many cases— killed (Bratton and Masunungure, 2006).

Before going into further detail on how this mutual dependency works, there is a need for clarity concerning who is assumed to belong to the ruling clique and what their respective roles are. The clique consists of just a handful of people who were formerly assembled in the so-called Joint Operational Command (JOC). This institution consisted of the top-rank officials responsible for the security sector.[2] Members are the Chief of the Army Constantine Chiwenga, the Chief of the Air Force, Perence Shiri, the former commander of the army, Solomon Mujuru, called Rex Nhongo during the liberation fight, the incumbent Minister of Defence, Emmerson Mnangagwa, the head of the CIO, Happyton Bonyongwe, the Head of State Security, Didymus Mutasa, the Prison Services Commissioner, Paradzayi

Zimondi, and the Commissioner General of the Police, Augustine Chihuri. Besides, the Reserve Bank Governor, Gideon Gono, was reportedly a member of JOC.

Shiri in particular was responsible for the atrocities committed by Mugabe's government. He was the commander of the North Korean-trained 5th Brigade, which is responsible for the actions in Matabeleland in the 1980s, when an estimated 18,000 people died due to state terrorism (Chan, 2003, pp. 25–33). Emmerson Mnangagwa is also viewed as brutal. Most Zimbabweans regard him 'as the architect of the pre-election military campaign [in 2008] that killed as many as 100 opposition supporters and displaced tens of thousands more; for ZANU-PF loyalists on the contrary, Mnangagwa is a sort of saviour' (*Africa Confidential*, 5 September 2008, p. 5).

The First Lady Grace Mugabe and the Attorney General, Johannes Tomana, also deserve explicit mention. Both gather, filter and provide the information available to the President. Mugabe alienated himself from the ordinary Zimbabwean a long time ago. Heidi Holland (2008) describes Mugabe as an unsociable person. He lives in relative isolation and is distant from the public. A former member of Mugabe's staff, interviewed by the author of this paper, characterises the President as a person who keeps his distance and with whom it is difficult to form a friendship. A fellow combatant during the liberation war shares this opinion by stressing the distance Mugabe keeps between himself and others (also see Tekere, 2006). The First Lady and the Attorney General might take advantage of this characteristic. The Attorney General in particular, an 'anti-MDC lawyer' (*The Star*, 27 January 2009, p. 1), has a strong influence when it comes to implementing government policies. 'He has total control over what the President hears and sees, and he also has total control over what goes out and whether it gets out or whether he actually bins it into file 13', states an anonymous interviewee. In fact, Tomana was, and still is, influential. He was considered as a 'key political weapon for the President to harass MDC figures with spurious charges and to hold them in custody for months. He is understood to be behind a plan to whittle away the MDC's majority in Parliament' (*The Times*, 22 May 2009, p. 46). A Western diplomat said that 'the attorney general makes sure there is no progress in the rule of law; . . . makes sure people remain arrested, or even get arrested; . . . also ensures that there are further land seizures, etc.' Shortly after the new government was sworn in, 'Tsvangirai acknowledge[d] that getting rid of Gono and the attorney general, Johannes Tomana, who has abused the law to lock up Mugabe's opponents, will be seen as an early test of his power' (*The Guardian*, 14 February 2009, p. 30). The MDC explicitly called for Tomana and Gono—the 'hard-liners a threat to transition'—to leave office (*Business Day*, 24 March 2009), indicating the influential role both played in sabotaging the new government.

Gono is able to control the political arena of Zimbabwe. One of Mugabe's former members of staff remarks that the Reserve Bank Governor has free rein. In fact, Gono controls the national budget and the money to be spent by the government. Gono managed to build a patronage system that even rivals Mugabe's (*Africa Confidential*, 5 September 2008). The last Mugabe administration had 'sat in their offices, but everything they wanted to do, every expense etc. has had to go through the Reserve Bank—through Gono and his team. So what has happened: the Reserve Bank has become a *de facto* government', remarks a well-informed source. The power that comes with Gono's position becomes obvious when walking through the city centre of Harare; the Reserve Bank is by far the most impressive building, taller than any other building in the city centre, symbolising the role of the Reserve Bank and its Governor.

The MDC tried to reduce Gono's influence by appointing Tendai Biti as Minister of Finance. Their personalities soon clashed in a fight about who would control the budget. Biti described 'Gono as an "Al-Qaeda"-like official deserving to be put before a firing squad for his activities as central bank governor' (*The Zimbabwe Independent*, 20–26 February 2009, p. 1). As Gono was favoured by Mugabe, it appeared that Biti was unlikely to win this fight. Ultimately, it is Gono, with the power to decide how much money flows to each ministry, who can influence policy-making. His room for manoeuvre became more limited when it was decided that the country's own currency should be replaced by foreign currencies.[3] Yet he remains influential. A scholar at the University of Zimbabwe seen as a fierce critic of Mugabe observed: 'Whatever little money there is, Gideon Gono is holding on to it as much as possible while his future is being determined, whether he will in fact continue as Governor of the Reserve Bank or maybe asked to step down'. A well-informed source emphasised that: 'if he [Gono] is not removed the Unity Government will fall apart, purely because it will be unworkable'. Yet, in February 2009 the aforementioned scholar remarked that it looked 'like he is very much going to stay in place. There will be a lot of work to be done between him and the Minister of Finance in order to reconcile them. But it's not going to be easy.' He was proved to be right.

Gono's crucial role became apparent when the EU made clear that it would provide financial aid only on Gono's replacement. A cabinet member stated: 'They [the Europeans] are so focused on the event of Gideon Gono going—as if that's going to deliver! You could get rid of Gono and get someone even worse in his place.' Europe's demand put Tsvangirai in a difficult position, limiting his possibilities because Mugabe would not have accepted Gono's resignation. Tsvangirai and Biti, however, needed Gono to resign as proof to the donor countries that the new government was serious about political transition. On the other hand, Tsvangirai could not run the risk of breaking up the government after having been in power for a few weeks, which meant that Mugabe and Gono emerged as the winners of the dispute. As a matter of fact, Gono still holds his position today. The London-based *Observer* reported in March 2010 that 'Zanu leaders have made it clear in private that there will be no concessions over replacing the central bank governor or attorney general until sanctions—which are hitting party grandees in their own pockets—are lifted' (*The Observer*, 2 March 2010, p. 18).

The roles played by the heads of the different security organs are self-evident: the police forces, the army and the CIO all control the state domestically. These three organs each bring fear to the population. The chief of the prisons controls the political prisoners. All members of the former JOC are dedicated members of ZANU-PF. Most of them refused to join the swearing-in ceremony of the new Prime Minister Tsvangirai. Some made strong statements prior to the inauguration that they would never attend such an event (*The Observer*, 15 February 2009). In particular, 'Chiwenga and ... Zimondi vowed ahead of the March 2008 synchro-nised polls that they would not salute the MDC-T [MDC under Tsvangirai] leader should he win the presidential election' (*The Financial Gazette*, 19–25 February 2009, p. 1).

The Mutual Dependency between ZANU-PF and Mugabe

On one particular occasion prior to the 2008 election and the inauguration of the new government Mugabe faced a serious threat from within his own party. This incident became known as 'the Tsholotsho conspiracy'. In November 2004 six out of the ten ZANU-PF provincial chairmen met in Tsholotsho to plan the future leadership composition of ZANU-PF.[4] Mugabe was warned about the 'conspiracy' (*Africa Confidential*, 3 December 2004) and suspended the six provincial chairmen from the ZANU-PF. This reaction highlights the seriousness of the incident. Jonathan Moyo, the then Information Minister, is thought to have organised the meeting (*Africa Confidential*, 17 December 2004). Observers also assume that he was assisted by Emmerson Mnangagwa. In fact, Moyo would have been promoted to Vice-President of the country (challenging Mugabe's favourite Joice Mujuru). Moyo was later expelled from the party and was voted into parliament as an independent candidate in 2005. Mnangagwa, on the contrary, managed to climb the ZANU-PF hierarchy again, making an 'impressive political comeback' (*Africa Confidential*, 9 May 2008, p. 6) and winning Mugabe's favour again. He was welcomed back into the JOC in early 2009, arguably because Mugabe depended on his patrons as much as they depended on him, particularly on a crucial figure like Mnangagwa.

However, after the Tsholotsho debacle, Mugabe was certainly aware of his unpopularity. Therefore, all close observers are convinced that Mugabe wanted to step down after the first round of the presidential election in 2008 when he suffered a defeat (*Mail & Guardian* online, 4 April 2008). A formerly close ally of Mugabe commented that 'he [Mugabe] probably would have welcomed the idea that he could exit with dignity and retire. But I don't believe the people he brought into powerful positions, particularly the military and the police, would have allowed him to leave.'

If Mugabe was prepared to step down under the condition that he would be granted amnesty, as the *Mail & Guardian* reported on 4 April 2008, why did he agree to join the Inclusive Government? There are arguably three main reasons. First, although he felt defeated, he was still aiming to fulfil his lifetime goal of dying in office (also see Dowden, 2006, p. 286). A second reason is that the JOC members were worried about their future. They wanted to keep up the status quo, i.e. having influence, holding power and maintaining a certain standard of living. An interviewee expressed this phenomenon in the slogan 'today I am a minister, tomorrow I starve'. Third, amnesty would be granted only to Mugabe, not to his cronies. Hence the ruling clique needed Mugabe to stay in power so that they could remain safe from the fear of prosecution. They probably felt insecure about their future, as no one spoke about a general amnesty at that stage. An international tribunal may have been established, which would have brought to light every unlawful action of the 29 years since ZANU-PF came to power. An alternative route, a truth and reconciliation commission, would also have been painful for the perpetrators, as shown by the experiences of neighbouring South Africa. In short, the ruling clique felt threatened. Their absence from Tsvangirai's swearing-in ceremony and their anti-MDC rhetoric indicate how much they wanted to maintain the status quo.

They needed Mugabe and Mugabe needed them. The President was certainly aware that he would be in serious trouble if he surrendered without ensuring the security and survival of the ruling clique; they would have found a way to hold him responsible for his command, particularly with regard to the ethnic cleansing in Matabeleland in the 1980s and Operation Murambatsvina in 2005.

In the end, as a collective body, they saw no other option than to rig the vote count from the first round of the presidential election, winning time and ultimately ensuring Mugabe's victory in the run-off.[5] This strategy paid off. It remains unclear whether Tsvangirai's withdrawal from the run-off was planned; however, the ruling clique was certainly pleased that it could maintain its democratic façade.

Shortly after having 'won' the election and having been hurriedly sworn in, Mugabe rushed to the African Union Summit, which took place in Sharm El-Sheikh in July 2008, to gain legitimacy from Africa's leaders. Despite some criticism, particularly from Mugabe's 'most effective opponent' (*Washington Post*, 2 July 2008, p. 6), Zambia's President Levy Mwanawasa, legitimacy was widely granted to Mugabe (*The Times*, 2 July 2008, p. 32; Welz and Junk, 2009).

The Weakness of the MDC and its Leadership

Mugabe's biggest advantage in the first 100 days of the new government was the weakness of the former opposition. The MDC leadership was not able to transform its overwhelming popularity into political power. The prevailing weakness of the MDC centres around two facts. First, the MDC is split into two camps: one is headed by Prime Minister Tsvangirai, the other by Deputy Prime Minister Arthur Mutambara. Second, Tsvangirai proved to be manipulable by being indecisive, not being able to say 'no', and being ill-advised.[6] This became apparent when the MDC entered the Inclusive Government. Mugabe explored every possibility in order to keep a grip on power. The distribution of ministerial posts (both sides got the same number of ministers) clearly shows how Mugabe managed to secure power for his party although ZANU-PF had lost the parliamentary election in March 2008 and Mugabe had gained fewer votes in the first round of the presidential election. Further indications of Tsvangirai's weakness are that the detention of Roy Bennett, the designated Deputy Minister of Agriculture, did not spark off any loud protest and there were no consequences when Mugabe did not respond to an ultimatum issued by Tsvangirai in May 2009. These themes will be elaborated on next.

The MDC emerged from the trade union movement (Raftopoulos, 2001, pp. 14–21). It was founded in 1999 but its origins date back earlier. The MDC split in 2005 when there was a dispute within the party about whether to participate in the Senate election. Mugabe had proposed to reinstate the Senate as a political organ of the country. Some MDC members saw it as a chance to participate in the election; others considered it a trap by Mugabe to strengthen his power base. At first, Tsvangirai lobbied to participate in the election. He was already promising Senate seats to members of the MDC. A well-known MP and MDC member of Mutambara's faction recalls:

> He [Tsvangirai] was quite in favour of the Senate at the time. Then something happened. He met Mujuru in South Africa...He came back...and started lobbying the entire party that we should not participate in the Senate election....So he changed his mind—we understand there was a lot of money which changed hands, but that's by the way...Finally we had a National Council Meeting to decide whether we are going to participate in this election or not. And eventually, because we couldn't come to a consensus, Tsvangirai in his ignorance perhaps—looking back—decided that we would vote on it...It was a secret vote and the result of the vote was 33 to participate in the election and 31 against and two spoiled papers. Now, the two spoiled papers:...one of them had a very small cross in the yes section...They said it was too small so it was considered spoiled. And the other one had written 'yes' instead of putting a cross...it was also considered spoiled even though in fact it was indicated clearly that the person wanted to participate. So the actual result should have been 35 against 31. But even 33, it was clear that we should participate in the Senate election. Tsvangirai then stood up in that meeting and said, well you have voted and you have voted to participate, but I do not believe that this is the best thing for the country and as your President I am going to overturn your vote and I am going out of here and announcing to the world that the MDC is not going to participate in this election...We couldn't believe...that this man can do this...He went out. He had organised a press conference at his house with all the international press and he lied to these people in front of the CNN and BBC cameras and so on. He said, our national council has voted and the vote was equal yes and no and I used my casting vote as President to say we will not participate in the election. First of all the vote wasn't equal and secondly under our constitution as a party, he didn't have a casting vote as President. There was not such provision in our party constitution. So he lied to the international community.

If this story is true, it reveals that Tsvangirai may not be as committed to democratic principles as one might assume. Despite personally having faced the brutal terror—including severe injuries—during campaigns by Mugabe loyalists in 2007 (see e.g. *The Guardian*, 19 March 2007, p. 19), he still did not adhere to the majority vote. Asked about Tsvangirai's commitment to democratic principles, an MDC member of cabinet said in February 2010:

> I think that Morgan Tsvangirai has come a long way since 2005, when the split occurred. All of us have learnt the lessons of that and have been sobered by the terrible things that have happened in this country not just before 2005 but since 2005 and especially in 2008. And in all my dealings with Morgan Tsvangirai in the last two months, I have to say that I have growing confidence in his commitment to democracy. I have been impressed by the way he has handled a variety of things.

The story about Roy Bennett's detention highlights Tsvangirai's weakness. Roy Bennett is a dispossessed white farmer who, due to political tensions, went to South Africa and while still in exile was assigned the post of Deputy Minister of Agriculture. When returning from South Africa to be sworn in, he was arrested by the security forces on treason charges. Bennett's inauguration was postponed for weeks while he was still held by the security organs. The incident uncovered a 'lack of sincerity on part of the ZANU-PF and the security forces the party controls' (*Zimbabwe Independent*, 20–26 February 2009, p. 16).

Taking Mugabe's display of strength into account, it would perhaps have been logical for the MDC to pull out of government. However, the Prime Minister refused to withdraw from the Inclusive Government, perhaps because 'he cannot say "no"', as one of this allies put it. Indeed, Tsvangirai is seen as indecisive (see also *Africa Research Bulletin*, 2007, p. 17145A). He did not consider the Bennett incident as a serious setback. The arrest 'undermines the spirit of our agreement' he said, continuing on to say that 'it is very important to maintain the momentum of our agreement' (*The Star*, 16 February 2009, p. 6). The new Prime Minister seemed to be committed to the power-sharing agreement and had lost sight of the fact that ZANU-PF loyalists took advantage of him. In May 2009, 100 days into the new government, a final conclusion on the Bennett case had not been drawn. Tsvangirai admitted that it was indeed 'a slow and frustrating process' (*The Times*, 22 May 2009, p. 46). In early 2010, Bennett was still unable to take up to his position of Deputy Minister of Agriculture (*The Observer*, 2 March 2010, p. 18).

Tsvangirai's weakness is shown not just by the Bennett case. To take another example, he sent an ultimatum to Mugabe on 22 April 2009 because Mugabe did not review his decision regarding the unilateral appointment of Gideon Gono and because land was still being seized (*Mail & Guardian* online, 22 April 2009). Mugabe, however, did not respond with any change to his policy. As Tsvangirai's tactical manoeuvre was ultimately not successful his party in turn set him an ultimatum to resolve the issues, causing disagreement within the government. 'While some senior MDC officials, especially members of the party's parliamentary caucus, were beginning to demand a pull-out from the government, Biti said this was not an option' (*Business Day*, 7 May 2009). Despite the increasing pressure on Tsvangirai and his leadership style, he stayed in government without having resolved the problems relating to the power-sharing agreement.[7]

In this context, it is worth asking who advised Tsvangirai in his first weeks in office. When Mugabe suggested that Tsvangirai was massively influenced by the British government, he did not seem to be completely wrong. Taylor and Williams (2002) argue that the role the former colonial power can play is limited, particularly with reference to the ZANU-PF regime. Yet, Britain could and certainly did influence Zimbabwe's political dynamics by supporting the MDC. In fact, the British and the US-American embassies in Harare seem to have played a crucial role in advising the MDC leader. Behind closed doors it is said that they were opposed to the power-sharing agreement. With regard to that agreement, the *Independent* argued in September 2008 that the British and US-American governments 'will be disappointed that Mr Mugabe still wields so much power' (*The Independent*, 13 September 2008, p. 28). A senior Western diplomat emphasised that there were clear signs that the Americans in particular were furious when Tsvangirai joined the Unity

Government in February 2009 under conditions dictated by President Mugabe. Europe's position in this context was not quite clear; however, there are indications that the Europeans, including Britain and Switzerland, were also against the power-sharing agreement. They thought it would be a false move for the MDC. Once Tsvangirai was sworn in, the Europeans had to adapt their strategies in the turbulent waters of Zimbabwe's policy while continuing to support Tsvangirai.

Some Western diplomats pointed out that the new government lacked experience in ruling a country, some even going so far as to say that Tsvangirai and the new government simply had 'no clue', which is not completely untrue. One might not go that far; however, taking into account that the new government had no experience in heading a state administration, in implementing policy, or even in running a party, (the MDC, for example, is better described as a loose structure than a well-organised body), there is some truth in the Western diplomats' claim. In addition to this, on the whole the new ministers found their staff to be disloyal.

The outlook for the MDC was bleak. *The Times* drew an interesting parallel between the MDC leader and Joshua Nkomo, who led the other liberation movement besides ZANU-PF in the 1970s and 1980s, which was later absorbed within ZANU-PF. This observation summarises the arguments made above and concludes this section:

> The Godfather of Zimbabwean politics was simply following the advice of the fictional Mafia boss Vito Corleone to 'keep your friends close and your enemies closer.' Mr Mugabe had executed exactly the same manoeuvre with Joshua Nkomo and his ZAPU party. The two former guerrilla commanders became bitter rivals after independence. Eventually, Mr Mugabe offered Mr Nkomo a place in government. In reality, he emasculated his opponent and ZAPU was swallowed up with one gulp by ZANU-PF. Mr Tsvangirai's detractors will argue that he has fallen into the same trap. Now that he has agreed to work with Mr Mugabe he has lost his moral authority and will no longer win support from his friends in the West. (*The Times*, 14 February 2009, p. 14)

The Other Players

The political landscape in Zimbabwe does not consist only of ZANU-PF and the MDC. There are more players involved in the political arena. Four groups will be outlined briefly as they are considered to play a crucial role. They are the (evicted) farmers, the trade unions, the businessmen, and the political grouping around ZANU-PF dissident Simba Makoni.

It is wrong to assume that Zimbabwe's farmers are united; they are organised in two rival groups. On the one hand, there is the Commercial Farmers Union (CFU); on the other hand, there is a group called Justice for Agriculture (JAC). The latter split away from the CFU for various reasons, most notably because they felt that their interests were not protected by the CFU, as JAC staff pointed out in interviews in their inconspicuous office in Harare. According to JAC, their organisation has more members than the CFU. JAC's members are mostly evicted farmers, whereas the CFU is primarily made up of current farmers. JAC has developed over the past months, appearing to be a human rights organisation at the beginning of 2009, rather than merely a pressure group for evicted farmers. JAC claims to be financed 40% by its members and 60% by 'the international community', although it was not revealed who was meant by that phrase. JAC is a highly political organisation, whereas the CFU only attempts to be political, with a President who was evidently proud to be invited by Robert Mugabe to the inauguration of the new government. JAC's claim not to be linked to any political party seems to be true. The CFU, on the other hand, was highly active in lobbying ZANU-PF and the MDC, as well as Simba Makoni. It is noteworthy that the latter is reportedly a member of the CFU. The CFU claimed 'to be kicked by all sides', but in fact the same CFU tried to gain the upper hand in the game by attempting to work with the other players to ensure the union's survival. Moreover, some members of the CFU leadership openly state that they want to join the new administration.

In short, the farmers, whether part of JAC or the CFU, were involved in the political scene in Zimbabwe. Whereas the one group seemed to work like a benevolent charity organisation, the other was struggling for survival. The land issue currently is and will be *the* domestic issue in Zimbabwe in the years to come. During the first 100 days of the Inclusive Government, farms were still being seized and Mugabe declared on his birthday in late February that 'land distribution will continue!' (*The Economist*, 7 March 2009, p. 40). There is little doubt that this will be the case and thus JAC and the CFU will remain important players.

The trade unions are difficult to judge. They claim not to be linked with one specific party. There is, however, no doubt that the Zimbabwe Congress of Trade Unions (ZCTU) is more closely linked to the MDC than to other parties. The MDC emerged from the labour and trade union movement. Morgan Tsvangirai has held the position of Secretary General of ZCTU. He and the current Secretary General are still in close contact. It is interesting that the latter (despite being leader of the self-proclaimed independent trade unions) was reported to be considered for the office of the next Governor of Harare (*Zimbabwe Independent*, 20–26 February 2009, p. 4).

The trade unions remain strong because they are well-organised at the grassroots level. It is no coincidence that the MDC emerged from this structure, as the trade unions served as a platform to discuss political issues during Zimbabwe's one-party era, which ended in the late 1990s. The impact that the local trade union structure has on the political opinion of the country must not be underestimated. Since the beginning of the millennium, ZANU-PF has perceived the labour movement as a threat, banning national strikes and threatening to imprison its organisers (Meredith, 2002, p. 162).

The next crucial players to be looked at are a handful of white businessmen with whom even Mugabe collaborates (see e.g. *Africa Confidential*, 3 April 2009). The stories about them are reminiscent of Hollywood movies, full of conspiracy and criminal activity; they are involved in the arms trade and the exploitation of natural resources, particularly in the Democratic Republic of Congo. Some of them are banned from travelling to the European Union and the United States and they are under scrutiny by Interpol. Although much of their racketeering remains secret and will probably continue to be so, there is no doubt that they influence politics in Zimbabwe. Their network is huge and their influence massive. One of the businessmen tried to become involved in the political arena by sponsoring the Tsholotsho meeting (*Africa Confidential*, 3 December 2004); but the same man seems to have links with Mugabe as well. Arguably, the business of these individuals is possible only under non-democratic conditions, where the rule of law is not respected. Therefore, they have a strong interest in maintaining the status quo. There are good reasons to assume that they support ZANU-PF individuals, as the involvement with the Tsholotsho meeting suggests.

The last important player is the political grouping of Simba Makoni, who is a highly ambivalent political figure. He had decided to leave the Mugabe administration and run for President in the 2008 election. However, he did not succeed, as he faced Mugabe and Tsvangirai as his opponents with greater popular support. Some observers argue that he only ran as candidate to divert votes from the opposition camp while keeping ties with ZANU-PF. In early March 2008, it was speculated that Makoni had the support of senior ZANU-PF members, most notably Vice-President Joice Mujuru and her husband, retired army commander Solomon Mujuru (*The Guardian*, 3 March 2008, p. 24). The fact that Mugabe did not criticise Makoni publicly is noteworthy, particularly when compared with the harsh rhetoric he used *vis-à-vis* the MDC.

After the Inclusive Government was established, Makoni and some of his loyalists claimed that they wanted to found a new party. A representative of the grouping said that they hoped to become the lucky third when the ZANU-PF/MDC coalition breaks apart. He explained the opportunity: 'you must be on the right side . . . everyone has his agenda'. The Makoni people claimed to be committed to ZANU-PF's original principles, which are rooted in the liberation struggle. They argued that Mugabe's party had strayed away from the original principles they had at independence and in the early years of the Republic of Zimbabwe. ZANU-PF claims to be left-wing; however, the party is far more conservative than they think. Makoni and his allies want to go back to the principles that ZANU-PF had initially fought for during the liberation struggle.

Conclusion

The analysis above has revealed that the situation in Zimbabwe was highly complex in the first 100 days of the Inclusive Government and continues to be so. There are many outstanding issues. Many different players were involved in the political setting; all had and still have their own agenda. Some proved to be very influential in the conduct of policy, most notably the JOC members. Although this policy-making unit was officially disbanded under the power-sharing agreement between the MDC and ZANU-PF, it is assumed that they still influence current policy-making and implementation. Mugabe can rely on the support of his allies, both within ZANU-PF and internationally, as shown by the fact that Mugabe is still in power. A Tsholotsho debacle is unlikely to happen again, as even Mugabe's ZANU-PF internal opposition became aware that they need Mugabe to remain in power. In the regional setting, South Africa protects Mugabe; in the global one, China played this role by vetoing decisions against Zimbabwe in the United Nations Security Council (Welz & Junk, 2009). One of Mugabe's biggest strategic advantages is the weakness of the former opposition. Tsvangirai is backed by the masses; however, he is not able to transform this support into bargaining power against Mugabe. Tsvangirai's ultimatums[8] were ignored by Mugabe, most notably the ultimatum issued in

April 2009. Tsvangirai seems to obey Mugabe's every command. The latter and his cronies control most key policies, such as state security and the economy. With it they control the public and the financial resources of the new government, thus having the power to sabotage the Inclusive Government. The staffs of the ministries largely comprise ZANU-PF members who show little loyalty to their new ministers. After 100 days in office, the prospects of the new government were bleak. The current political situation shows that a deep transition has not yet taken place. The problems are too deep-rooted and complex and therefore difficult to overcome.

Acknowledgements

This article is based on primary research conducted in Zimbabwe in February 2009 with the generous funding of the Centre of Excellence 'Cultural Foundation of Integration' at the University of Konstanz. The author is especially thankful to Emily, Fabian, Hubertus, Timothy and Christina. The author would also like to thank Stephen Chan for his helpful comments on earlier drafts of this paper. Some interviews were conducted anonymously owing to the harsh political conditions in Zimbabwe.

Notes

1. For a quantitative study based on Afrobarometer data, see Michael Bratton and Eldred Masunungure (2006).
2. It is not known exactly who is a member of the JOC (see *The Observer*, 15 February 2009 and *The Zimbabwe Times*, 12 August 2008). The presented list includes all names that were mentioned in the interviews conducted in Harare.
3. US dollars and the South African rand are mostly used. Additionally, Botswana's pula, the euro and the UK's pound are also used.
4. For more details on the Tsholotsho conspiracy, see *Africa Confidential*, 3 and 17 December 2004. For Jonathan Moyo's perspective of the incident, see www.prof-jonathan-moyo.com
5. According to the above, there are reasons to assume that policy-making in the JOC after the March 2008 election followed what Janis (1972) describes as 'group think.' Everyone was committed, dissidents were excluded and decisions had to be made quite rapidly. This is, however, to be understood as a footnote, and requires further research.
6. In an interview with the German-based *Frankfurter Allgemeine Zeitung* (21 November 2008, p. 7), Tsvangirai admitted that the MDC had made too many compromises, although they won the election. ('Wir haben schon so viele Kompromisse gemacht. Wir haben die Wahl gewonnen und Mugabe erlaubt, an der Macht zu bleiben. Wir können nicht bis zur Kapitulation mit ihm verhandeln.')
7. The sudden death of Tsvangirai's wife in a tragic car accident certainly did not help Tsvangirai to adopt a firmer position towards President Mugabe.
8. Tsvangirai issued a 24-hour ultimatum to Mugabe on 26 June 'to negotiate or face being shunned as an illegitimate leader' (*Mail & Guardian* online, 26 June 2008).

References

Africa Confidential (2004) Zimbabwe: bye-bye, Moyo, 3 December, p. 8.
Africa Confidential (2004) Zimbabwe: a heartbeat away, 17 December, p. 1.
Africa Confidential (2008) Mnangagwa's return to form, 9 May, p. 6.
Africa Confidential (2008) It's go-go with Gono, 5 September, p. 5.
Africa Confidential (2008) Mnangagwa's second coming, 5 September, p. 5.
Africa Confidential (2009) Zimbabwe: Bredenkamp bites back, 3 April, p. 12.
Africa Research Bulletin (2007) Zimbabwe: political fissures, 1–31 July, pp. 17143A–17145C.

Bratton, M. and Masunungure, E. (2006) Popular reactions to state repression: Operation Murambatsvina in Zimbabwe, *African Affairs*, 16(422), pp. 21–45.

Chan, S. (2003) *Robert Mugabe: A Life of Power and Violence* (Ann Arbor: University of Michigan Press).

Dowden, R. (2006) Engaging with Mugabe, *The Round Table*, 95(384), pp. 283–286.

Gevisser, M. (2008) *Thabo Mbeki: The Dream Deferred* (Cape Town: Jonathon Ball) (updated international edition).

Holland, H. (2008) *Dinner with Mugabe: The Untold Story of a Freedom Fighter who became a Tyrant* (Johannesburg: Penguin).

Janis, I. (1972) *Victims of Groupthink: A Psychological Study of Foreign Policy Decisions and Fiascos* (Boston: Houghton Mifflin).

Meredith, M. (2002) *Mugabe: Power and Plunder in Zimbabwe* (Oxford: Public Affairs).

Raftopoulos, B. (2001) The Labour Movement and the emergence of opposition politics in Zimbabwe, in B. Raftopoulos and L. Sachikonye (Eds), *Striking Back: The Labour Movement and the Post-colonial State in Zimbabwe 1980–2000* (Harare: Waever Press).

Taylor, I. and Williams, P. (2002) The limits of engagement: British foreign policy and the crisis in Zimbabwe, *International Affairs*, 78(3), pp. 547–566.

Tekere, E. (2006) *A Lifetime for Struggle* (Harare: SAPES).

Welz, M. and Junk, J. (2009) Zimbabwe still at the crossroad? Domestic stalemate, regional appeasement, and international half-heartedness, *Sicherheit und Frieden—Security and Peace*, 27(3), pp. 185–194.

Lessons from African Diplomatic Initiatives in the Democratic Republic of Congo, Sudan and Zimbabwe

SYDNEY MUFAMADI
Minister of Provincial and Local Government, Government of South Africa, South Africa

ABSTRACT *'Be robust, be tough on self-serving tyrants whose hands are dripping with the blood of their own people.' This has been the mantra chanted with quasi-religious conviction, directed at leaders of South Africa, the Southern African Community and the African Union. Proponents of this doctrine of coercive diplomacy are moved by a spirit that connects humanitarian intervention to regime change and the rights of democratic states to replace illiberal tyrants in the name of both the victims and the wider call of security for the ethically superior liberal parts of the world. This article examines the comparative utility of the approach outlined above vis-à-vis an approach that privileges suasion and engagement over confrontation. Serving as a representative case study for this comparison are three African countries, which have been mired in conflicts that led to untold human suffering: the Democratic Republic of Congo, Sudan and Zimbabwe. The article argues that not only do proponents of coercive diplomacy fundamentally misconceive the political dynamics of the countries, region and continent in which they are seeking to intervene, but also that rather than providing an answer to the problem at hand, their tough posture is at best ineffective and at worst counter-productive. Indeed, experience in these countries, and in others such as Angola, Namibia, Mozambique and South Africa before them, challenges the universality of diplomatic approaches and assumptions that deify coercive diplomacy as a means of solving conflicts. The article concludes by elaborating on the nuances of the competing diplomatic approaches. These nuances, as well as the evidence culled from the three experiences, buttress the author's view that the people and governments of Africa share with the rest of the world a desire for a conflict-free continent and a peaceful world. As they increase their agency for bringing this result about, they require and deserve to be supported by the rest of the world.*

Introduction

It may be useful to set out briefly the histories of each of the three cases examined, namely, the Democratic Republic of Congo (DRC), Sudan and Zimbabwe.

Democratic Republic of Congo

A former Belgian colony at the heart of Africa, the DRC attained independence in 1960. Manipulated decolonisation helped feed the rise of President Mobutu. Since the country attained independence, it has experienced occasional outbreaks of civil war as a result of the factional scramble for the accumulation of profit from extracting coltan and other mineral resources.

Not only was the existence of mineral resources exploited by endogenous Congolese warring factions, but some neighbouring countries such as Rwanda, Uganda and other regional actors also joined the fray. Mobutu Sese Seko instrumentalised the Cold War by projecting himself as an ally of the West in its quest to contain the spread of Communism on the African continent. This relationship proved to be an important fulcrum of his political security and it saw him enjoying an uninterrupted tenure of political office (from the 1960s) until he was toppled in May 1997 by Laurent-Desire Kabila in a Rwanda/Uganda-backed rebellion. As soon as he had proclaimed himself the new President, Kabila reintroduced the flag and the currency unit originally adopted at independence, banned political parties and began to consolidate his power.

During Kabila's years in office, the DRC had been carved up by various neighbouring forces and its resources were looted by the occupying forces. The entire eastern half of the country was occupied by Ugandan, Rwandan and Burundian troops and various Congolese rebel forces with whom they had aligned themselves. In the other half of the Congo, the government was able to enjoy control only through the presence and support of troops from Zimbabwe, Angola, Namibia, and, to a lesser extent, Sudan and Chad.

Kabila fell out with Uganda and Rwanda, two of his allies that helped him come to power. Since that point, the DRC has been mired in an armed conflict that effectively started in August 1998.

The Organisation of African Unity (OAU) led a mediation effort that was launched in Lusaka, Zambia, in July 1999. It was here that the Lusaka Accord was adopted, calling for national dialogue between Kabila and the armed opposition groups, the Rally for a Democratic Congo (RCDL), the Movement for the Liberation of Congo (MLC) and the unarmed civilian opposition, the establishment of state administration throughout the country, and the creation of a new national army; the United Nations (UN) was asked to deploy a peace-keeping force to the DRC, in collaboration with the OAU. The UN was also asked to designate a neutral facilitator for the Inter-Congolese Dialogue (ICD). Sir Ketumile Masire was nominated as the facilitator of the ICD, which met in South Africa's Sun City from 25 February to 18 April 2002 and negotiated a power-sharing agreement between the main parties (although the RCD declined to sign).

Since the country attained independence in 1960, the ICD was the second time that the Congolese people had gathered to look at the way the country was governed. The first time was the 1991–92 national conference, which brought together all the political forces in the then Zaire to map out the future of the country. This process was scuttled by dictator Mobutu.

A process to reach an all-inclusive agreement to end the DRC conflict opened in Pretoria, South Africa, in October 2002. This process brought together representatives of the government, RCD-Goma, MLC, political opposition, civil society, RCD-ML, RCO-N and the Mai-Mai. Held under the mediation of the UN Secretary General's special Envoy, Moustapha Niasse, and a special envoy of the then President Thabo Mbeki, the present writer.

On 16 December 2002, the parties reached an agreement that was concluded within the spirit of inclusion, nation-building, accountability and respect for the territorial integrity of the DRC. The 'Global and All-inclusive Agreement on the Transition in the DRC' called for a two-year transition period, during which Joseph Kabila would remain President of the DRC and run the country with four vice-presidents—nominated, respectively, by the government, the DRC-Goma, the MLC and a member of the unarmed opposition. In addition, the agreement provided for:

(1) a transitional legislature made up of a National Assembly of 500 members and a Senate of 120 members;

(2) the creation of a united national army drawn from the government force, RCO-Goma forces, MLC forces, elements of the RCD-Liberation Movement, RCD-National and the Mai-Mai;

(3) a Superior Defence Council (*Counseil superieur de 10 Defense*) composed of the President, the four vice-presidents, the Minister of Defence, the Minister of Internal Affairs, the Minister of Foreign Affairs, the army Commander, and the Commander of the airforce, land force and the navy.

Zimbabwe

Zimbabwe achieved its independence in April 1980 following a 'negotiated' settlement, which the then Prime Minister of Britain, Margaret Thatcher, was authorised to initiate by the Commonwealth Prime Ministers' Conference that took place in Lusaka, Zambia, on 1 August 1979. Mrs Thatcher's brief was to involve all parties to the conflict in a settlement that would include framing a new constitution and would lead to free and fair elections supervised by Britain. The Commonwealth took responsibility for providing observers.

Agreement having been reached in Lusaka, Thatcher's designated Chairman of the round-table conference, Lord Carrington, published on 14 August 1979 *Draft Constitutional Proposals* and invited representatives of Zimbabwe-Rhodesia's Bishop Abel Muzorewa-led government as well as the leaders of the Zimbabwe African National Union (ZANU) and the Zimbabwe African People's Union (ZAPU) to attend. The two parties were, at the time, led respectively by Robert Mugabe and Joshua Nkomo.

The Lancaster Conference was opened on 10 September and culminated in an agreement between the parties, which, in essence, was an endorsement of Carrington's original plan. Carrington's draft constitutional proposals were accepted, and in addition, it was agreed that:

(1) Muzorewa would abdicate power, parliament would be dissolved and a British Governor would take overall charge of the transitional arrangement (transition towards elections);

(2)   the governor would be in control of all the armed forces in Rhodesia, including the Rhodesian Security Forces, the Auxiliaries and the guerrillas;
(3)   normal policing would be carried out by the existing police with the assistance of the Security Forces, if necessary.

The constitutional proposals, in addition to providing for free and fair elections, provided safeguards for minorities.

This agreement having been reached, the stage was set for the first ever democratic election, which was won by Robert Mugabe's ZANU. In that election, in a vote of confidence in Mugabe and Nkomo as the nation's liberators, the Patriotic Front (PF) won 77 seats, while Muzorewa's UANC could only get three seats. Mugabe formed his first government of the post-independence Zimbabwe, and in it he included members of Nkomo's ZAPU as well as elements from the party of Rhodesia's erstwhile Prime Minister, Ian Douglas Smith. The subsequent merger of ZANU and ZAPU allowed Mugabe, through a new political vehicle known as ZANU-PF, to consolidate power, first as the Prime Minister and later as the Executive President of Zimbabwe. Not only did he score landslide victories in subsequent elections, but also he increased his electoral majority each time he contested an election.

For a while after independence, Zimbabwe was a star-spangled post-colonial performer and an inspiring model of progressive change in Southern Africa. With its policy of national reconciliation, it had shown the way as it brought about a change for the better in areas such as education, health and rural development. Its regional and global prestige allowed it to play a significant role in facilitating the quest for peace and stability in Mozambique.

The following indices attest to the fact that, for a while, post-independence Zimbabwe was characterised by a positive change in the lives of the people of Zimbabwe:

(1)   In the period 1980–89, primary school enrolments rose from 1.2 million children to 2.2 million.
(2)   In the same period, secondary school enrolment grew from 74,000 to 671,000, a rate of expansion that was faster than any ever experienced anywhere else in the world.
(3)   Increased health expenditures resulted in such positive developments as an increase in life expectancy from 55 to 59 years.
(4)   State intervention aimed at encouraging rural development in the farmers' share of marketed maize rose from zero in 1980 to more than 70% in 1989.

The picture changed when a new political player, the Movement for Democratic Change (MDC), contested the 2000 parliamentary elections and achieved a representation significant enough to signal that the ruling party's grip on the legislative instrumentalities was loosening. The MDC garnered 47% of the vote and 57 seats, as opposed to ZANU-PF's 48.6%, which translated into 62 seats. This was followed by a Presidential election in 2002, which Mugabe won, defeating, among others, the MDC's Morgan Tsvangirai.

The aftermath of the 2000 elections was characterised by growing hostility between ZANU-PF and the MDC, with the parties trading invectives hitherto unseen in the country's political domain. There was also a growing indication (in the form of the banning of meetings of opposition parties, arrests of individuals, etc.) that the ruling party was closing the democratic space by resorting to the use of coercive instrumentalities of the state.

The space for meaningful dialogue between the parties also appeared to be non-existent because of the reigning atmosphere of paranoia that was created by the high-volume diplomacy of the major Western powers, which called for regime change and expressed overt support for the MDC. This allowed ZANU-PF to claim, with some measure of plausibility, that the MDC was a foreign implant whose delegated task it was to reverse the gains of the revolution. ZANU-PF charged that MDC was a creation, in particular, of a British government that wanted to evade its responsibility to confront its colonial legacy in Zimbabwe. This, they argued, had to do with the decision that was taken by Thatcher's Tory government to suspend its promotion of the land distribution programme as a rebuke to Mugabe for allegedly not accounting properly for UK taxpayers' funding. It is said that Thatcher's successor, John Major, subsequently patched up the relationship by promising to resume the land purchase deal on which Lancaster House's success had hinged 20 years earlier. ZANU-PF accused Tony Blair of, on the advice of his cabinet colleague Clare Short, simply dismissing the contention that the UK had an obligation to fund land redistribution. Blair is said to have argued that his Labour Party was not responsible for colonialism.

In an attempt to take the parties beyond the blame-game and focus them on the task of normalising the political and security situation in Zimbabwe, the Southern African Development Community (SADC) leaders resolved at their Extra-ordinary Summit held on 29 March 2007 in Dar-es-Salaam, Tanzania, to mandate the then President of South Africa, Thabo Mbeki, 'to continue to facilitate dialogue between the opposition and the Government'. The summit also appealed to Britain 'to honour its compensation obligations with regard to land reform made at the Lancaster House Conference', and it 'appealed for the lifting of all forms of sanctions against Zimbabwe'.

Sudan

Contemporary Sudan, Africa's largest country with a land area roughly the size of Western Europe, was first put together in the early 19th century under Turko-Egyptian rule. At independence in 1956, power was transferred from the British colonialists to a Riverine Arab minority that occupied a privileged position during the years of British colonialism. As the new ruling group, this minority used power to promote its exclusive interests, including its monopolisation of political power.

Today Khartoum and its environs are a middle-income enclave surrounded by peripheries that are among the least-developed areas on the planet. For more than 50 years, a dominant Khartoum elite has marginalised and repressed all others: Kardofanis and Darfurians, Christians and followers of traditional beliefs, the uneducated poor, Western, Eastern and Southern Sudanese alike.

The neglect of the peripheries is well depicted by conditions in the Southern Sudan region—a region that is considerably larger than neighbouring Kenya and is home to about 9 million people who are made up of more than 60 ethnic groups ranging from settled farming communities to pastoralists. A region without clearly defined borders and with weak institutions nevertheless oozes immense fertility. Yet expats in Juba drink Ceres-branded mango juice imported from Uganda while heaps of mangos are left rotting where they fall. It is here that 75% of Sudan's proven oil reserves of 6.3 billion barrels reposes.

Omar al-Bashir, Sudan's current President, seized power in 1989 and his government has since been embroiled in intermittent conflicts with various regions. The current war in Darfur is one such symptom of a fundamental division that has plagued Sudan since independence: the centre versus the periphery. Diplomatic initiatives aimed at bringing peace between the centre and the peripheries have produced a raft of negotiated agreements, which include: the Humanitarian Ceasefire Agreement of April 2004 (N'djamena); the Declaration of Principles for the Resolution of the Conflict in Darfur (DOP) of July 2005 (Abuja); the Darfur Peace Agreement (DPA) of May 2006 (Abuja); the Eastern Sudan Peace Agreement (ESPA) of October 2006 (Asmara); as well as the Comprehensive Peace Agreement (CPA) of January 2005 (Naivasha and Nairobi). Added to this is a report produced by the African Union High-level Panel on Darfur (2009), a panel chaired by South Africa's former President Mbeki and charged with the responsibility:

> to examine the (Darfur) situation in depth and submit recommendations to the African Union Peace and Security Council on how best the issues of accountability and combating impunity, on the one hand, and reconciliation and healing, on the other, could be effectively and comprehensively, addressed, including through the establishment of Truth and/or Reconciliation Commissions, with the active involvement of the AU [African Union] and its relevant institutions and, as necessary, the support of the larger international community.

After a substantive engagement with the people of Sudan, especially in Darfur, held over a period of six months, the panel unsurprisingly concluded that the crisis in Darfur ultimately has its roots in the five-decades-old civil war that engulfed the Sudan. Although there are elements of ethnic division to the battle to control the farming land—the nomads are primarily Arabs whereas the established farmers of Darfur are Africans—economic and political issues are at the heart of the political fighting. The various tribes in the region have found themselves in increasing competition for the same shrinking set of natural resources, including water, grassland and arable soil.

The risk of violence in a country with such an unstable political system and a history of inter-ethnic disputes is always present. In this regard, Sudan is indeed not a historical aberration, nor is the problem it faces a peculiarity of Africa. This problem was similarly experienced in places such as Rwanda and Yugoslavia.

The assignment given to the Panel was born out of the AU's desire to help find lasting peace to the Darfur armed conflict, which started in 2003 and has, according to estimates, caused approximately 14,000 deaths, possibly more. In 2009, the International Criminal Court in The Hague indicted President Bashir on seven counts of war crimes against humanity—making him the first sitting head of state to be indicted by the International Criminal Court. According to Sudan scholar Alex de Waal, the indictment was cathartic but counter-productive. De Waal believes that it (the indictment) offered Bashir no chance to compromise, while making him a champion of anti-Western defiance.

It will be remembered that some of the powerful Western lobbies have come to see intervention in Sudan as part of the War on Terror. These tend to manipulate genuine humanitarian crises such as the death of an estimated two million people in two civil wars between the South and the Northern government in 1955–72 and between 1983 and 2005, to imbricate what needs to be done in Sudan into the global War on Terror. These views undergird an intellectual climate where wild claims are made without recourse to empirical or historical perspective, e.g. casting the Sudan ruling elite as Islamic and therefore a terror threat. This explains why the United States, in its concern at the moment of transition to 2000 with 'Islamic terrorism', launched cruise missile attacks against targets in Sudan.

A look at Obama's Sudan strategy announced on 19 October 2009 suggests that de Waal's view found traction inside the White House. In terms of the strategy, Obama has favoured engagement over confrontation. The strategy encapsulates a new US approach to world affairs. It commits the administration to promoting efforts to end the fighting, to boost human rights, and long-term efforts to implement the CPA, the deal between the North and the South that ended their civil war in 2005. It is worth emphasising that the CPA identified key issues at the heart of both the Darfur conflict and many of Sudan's other internal divisions: the East, the Central-Southern states of Southern Kordofan and the Blue Nile. Obama's strategy is unfortunately weakened by dissenters inside his own administration. While the US Special Envoy to Sudan General Scott Gration favours engagement, the ambassador to the UN, Dr Susan Rice, is known to want more aggression.

In this regard, the approach taken by the Obama administration is consistent with the position of the AU High-level Panel on Darfur. The Panel recommended that all Sudanese formations (political and non-political), the African Union and the UN, must undertake a process of promoting peace among the Sudanese population and render violence less attractive as a means of achieving political objectives. In addition, the Panel recommended that the parties should draw up a political mobilisation plan to strengthen peace and unity in different parts of the country. The parties were also urged to integrate such a plan in the framework as well as the Global Political Agreements.

Atmospheric Prerequisites for Peace-making

In all cases cited above (i.e. the DRC, Sudan and Zimbabwe), South African diplomats were either acting as facilitators of national dialogue so designated by SADC or the AU, or as advisors to the continental body on the measures that could be introduced efficaciously to bring an end to hostilities and armed conflicts. This fact speaks to the growing determination on the part of the African leadership to turn the continent into a peaceful space of its own making.

Peace-making and conflict resolution initiatives have had to be undertaken amid an atmosphere that forecloses attempts to find negotiated settlements between the interlocutors. On the one hand, the incumbent regime, believing itself to be a victim of externally hatched schemes to remove it from power, is unable to set a new course that would make reconciliation with the interlocutors possible, let alone create conditions for the rise of a genuinely pluralistic society at peace with itself. These inhospitable circumstances issue from a discourse that presents the problem in either/or dichotomising tropes: the one side to the conflict is the devil-incarnate (the perpetrator), and the other is the paragon of political virtue (the victim). On this account, the sides are not *per se* made up of ordinary human beings who are locked in a complex set of relationships.

On the other hand, the oppositionist groups are made to see the 'international community' (in the form of foreign governments and non-governmental organisations) as the knighted saviour with unfettered capacity to bring about a solution. This tough posture that some in the international diplomatic community are wont to adopt is at best ineffective and at worst counter-productive. It fosters the mistaken belief on the part of the 'victims' that it is possible for them to realise a change for the better without having to contemplate a deal, which must constitute a positive-sum negotiated outcome.

The situation in the Western Sudanese region of Darfur illustrates the danger that repressed groups learn: the (negative) lesson that escalating confrontation might pay back in the long term. Apparently the same propaganda strategy 'proved' successful for Kosovo Albanians (and in part for Bosnian Muslims), who hoped to attract international sympathy and trigger intervention. Writing in the *New York Magazine* of 17 October 2004, Scott Anderson observed that oppositionist groups in Darfur expected that humanitarian reasons would prompt more assertive Western involvement, and thus created further conflict instead of limiting it. According to a state department official working in Sudan, the rebels have been very content to sit back, let the village burnings go on and let the killings go on because the more international pressure that is brought to bear on Khartoum, the stronger their position grows. The AU High-level Panel on Darfur encountered Darfurian civilians and cadres of the Justice and Equality Movement (JEM) who believed that NATO would one day intervene and remove the regime in Khartoum.

In circumstances such as prevail in Darfur the priorities of international diplomacy have to be:

(1) To end the (asymmetrical) violence as soon as possible and to separate physically the different factions on the ground.
(2) To improve the human condition by changing the structural conditions, which comprehensively addresses the underlying problems that led to the conflict. The programme must also spell out a support role to be played by the international community. Such a programme is visualised in the report of the AU High-level Panel on Darfur.

Pitfalls of Robust Mediation and Lessons for Zimbabwe

Besides the unnerving parallels that we see from the history of the unintended consequences of the rhetoric that promises robust intervention, the problem with exhortations for robust mediation is that this is an inherently undemocratic stipulation that attempts to impose a 'solution' prescribed by the mediator. It entails an a priori determination of the solution (by others), and a relegation of the preference of those affected to second-tier importance. In a letter to the leaders of the Zimbabwean parties dated 4 April 2007, the then SADC-designated facilitator of the Inter-Zimbabwean dialogue, Thabo Mbeki, made it clear that the Zimbabweans would be expected collectively to frame the agenda and negotiate the outcome of the talks. This approach is premised on the perspective that sees self-help solutions as having a better prospect of sustainability than externally imposed ones. The approach taken by SADC in this instance, and indeed in other instances, is different from Lord Carrington's Lancaster House approach in which the Chairman presents a draft constitution for comments and then proceeds to twist the arm of the 'negotiating parties' to accept the draft.

The SADC mediation effort in Zimbabwe sought to take the parties beyond the blame-game and focus them on the important task of formulating a roadmap for navigating the problems facing the country and the people. Among other things, the parties would, as they indeed did, negotiate and agree interim arrangements providing a framework for reforming the governing dynamics of Zimbabwe. These arrangements entail changing the visible institutions of the state and their interaction with society, and creating the basis for social trust. More importantly, the Global Political Agreement (GPA) commits the negotiating parties, working together with the rest of Zimbabwean society, to a process of driving this transformative undertaking.

Properly handled, this provision would enable the MDC formations and ZANU-PF to become champions of societal mobilisation—mobilising society behind and around the democratic perspectives encapsulated in the GPA. History teaches us that democratisation requires organisations of civil society to engage with state institutions in order to achieve their aims and improve their conditions of existence. Conditions for this to happen were laid down more effectively in the inter-Congolese Dialogue, where civil society organisations took part and the eventual agreement provided for their central involvement in the Human Rights Commission and other democracy-supporting institutions. Likewise, the extensive consultations carried out by the AU High-level Panel on Darfur involved all sections of society in their various formations.

State institutions must be shaped such that they are vested with the intrinsic possibility fully to penetrate society, mobilise resources, or ultimately engender legitimacy. The fact that the GPA was signed by ZANU-PF and the two MDC formations after a controversial Presidential election run-off that neither SADC nor the AU could recognise as the free expression of the will of the people of Zimbabwe is instructive. It ties up with the only message that could be divined from the outcome of the March 2008 electoral contest. The message was directed at all sides: 'You cannot bypass the others and still be able to achieve peace and stability in Zimbabwe'. This reality enjoins the parties to cooperate in a mutually transforming relationship that is premised on the understanding that:

(1) the parties face a common challenge;
(2) they need to develop a precise definition and shared understanding of this common challenge;

(3) they need to agree on the things that need to be done in order to produce a positive-sum landscape.

Although Zimbabwean civil society organisations did not take direct and active part in the dialogue, the facilitators did hold periodic briefing sessions with them and solicited their active counsel. Another consoling factor is that the negotiating parties themselves have a demonstrable elective base because they are the three major parties in parliament. Therein lies the source of legitimacy for such agreements and commitments as they make in the course of negotiations.

The Zimbabwean state is frequently the target of criticism from human rights groups and governments for allegedly violating human rights principles and norms. The same charges are levelled against the Sudanese state. This is the backdrop against which some in the international community deployed human and material resources towards mounting a high-volume campaign over Zimbabwe and Darfur. While such campaigns are legitimate and important, unfortunately in the case of Zimbabwe the combination of sanctions and rhetoric about regime change à la 'the Axis of Evil' served only to vindicate Harare's paranoia and reduce options available to the governments who advocate such measures.

For their part, African diplomats understand their political possibilities and the limits of coercive diplomacy. They orientate themselves on the approach that seeks slowly to build a culture of rights based on individual and state responsibility. Drawing from the experiences of earlier transition negotiations of the 1960s to the 1980s (including the transition from apartheid to democracy in South Africa in the 1990s), they resist the temptation to remove from the political sphere violent struggles for territory, resources or allegiances that are ordinarily regarded as political or sociological. They leave it to the negotiating parties to examine (in the course of dialogue) the historical and political context in which such violent hostilities occurred, and to decide what to do about it. Opening past activities of brutality and/or violations of human rights to discussion and possible scrutiny provides the means to avoid a recurrence.

Conclusion

A new mood is abroad on the African continent. It is a mood that embraces engagement over confrontation. This mood gives all people of goodwill reason to see the future through hopeful eyes. It speaks of Africa's determination to improve its agential power for solving its own problems. We see it in the drive to transform Sudan into the epicentre of a process of building a new world—a world in which Muslims, Christians and practitioners of traditional religious beliefs exist in conditions of reciprocity. This drive must be buttressed by such support as was manifest in the DRC where the rest of the international community was constituted (by agreement with the Congolese parties) into an international committee whose task it was to support the transition. This must be extended to supporting the process of post-conflict reconstruction and development.

Angola–Zimbabwe Relations: A Study in the Search for Regional Alliances

SABELO J. NDLOVU-GATSHENI

Department of Development Studies, University of South Africa, South Africa

ABSTRACT *The common approach to the study of foreign policies of Southern African Development Community (SADC) states is to locate them within the context of 'brother presidents' and 'sister liberation movements'. There is emphasis on liberation war camaraderie as a key variable. However, Angola–Zimbabwe (read as MPLA–ZANU-PF and MPLA–MDC) relations have no noticeable strong liberation war-time ties. The relations are traceable to the post-1980 period when the Zimbabwe African National Union–Patriotic Front (ZANU-PF) pursued a deliberate policy of integrating itself within the SADC region and this coincided with the Popular Movement for the Liberation of Angola's (MPLA) long-time desire to isolate its internal enemies of the National Front for the Liberation of Angola and the National Union for the Total Independence of Angola. What is also noticeable is the opacity and ambiguities in Angola–Zimbabwe relations, which have provoked growth of speculation and suspicion. The only time Angola and Zimbabwe openly collaborated was in their intervention in the Democratic Republic of Congo war in 1998 under the auspices of the SADC in general and the SADC Organ on Politics, Defence and Security in particular. However, two recent developments—the state visit to Luanda by the Prime Minister of Zimbabwe and the leader of the Movement for Democratic Change (MDC-T) Morgan Tsvangirai in October 2009, and the announcement by ZANU-PF of the China-Sonangol $8bn investment deal in November 2009—have provoked fresh interest in understanding Angola–Zimbabwe relations in the context of a regional initiative to resolve the Zimbabwe crisis. Although Angola is visible as a member of the SADC in the search for a solution to the Zimbabwe crisis, it has not openly expressed its foreign policy towards Zimbabwe. Unlike Botswana under Ian Khama and Zambia under the late Levy Mwanawasa, which openly criticised President Robert Mugabe and ZANU-PF over governance and its human rights record, Angola has remained quiet, making it hard to know its exact position vis-à-vis initiatives towards resolution of the Zimbabwe crisis. Interest in Angolan foreign policy is further motivated by the fact of its ascendancy as one of the regional powers; building on its rich mineral resources, it has the potential leverage to help in the resolution of the Zimbabwe crisis if it openly expressed its position. At the moment, it is not clear whether Angola has also adopted 'quiet diplomacy', just like South Africa under President Thabo Mbeki in its dealings with Zimbabwe.*

Introduction

Angola's foreign policy towards Zimbabwe has remained ambiguous and opaque. As a result, Angola–Zimbabwe relations are subject to widespread media speculation, particularly within Zimbabwe, and suspicion among opposition forces and civil society organisations concerned about democratisation and sincerity and impartiality of some regional powers to finding a resolution to the Zimbabwe crisis. This can be attributed to a number of factors. Angola, just like Zimbabwe, was born out of an armed liberation struggle and is headed by a president with the longest term of office in the region. This political reality might predispose the ruling Popular Movement for the Liberation of Angola (MPLA) party favourably towards the Zimbabwe African National Union–Patriotic Front (ZANU-PF) and President Robert Mugabe, who has been in power since 1980. Ever since Angola achieved its political independence in 1975, its foreign policy has been very complex, veering between a clearly pro-Soviet Union and Cuba stance and emphasising non-alignment as a key component of its external engagement. Ambiguity has always been a major component of Angola's foreign policy. Under both Agostinho Neto and Jose Eduardo Dos Santos presidencies, Angola has been run pretty much by a nationalist-military alliance with a civilian façade that was also manifest in Zimbabwe throughout the decade-long crisis. This shared organisational structure might influence affinity between MPLA and ZANU-PF. Both ZANU-PF and MPLA have maintained aspects of liberation war-time quasi-military qualities, including maintaining secret operations and linkages that are not part of public policy. Since the end of civil war in Angola in 2002, its foreign policy has looked east to China, a long-time ally of ZANU-PF, which since 1992 had been developing a 'Look East Policy' (Friedrich-Ebert-Stiftung, 2004). This Chinese connection can be another basis for MPLA–ZANU-PF cooperation and affinity.

Ambiguity in Angolan foreign policy also has to do with its identity crisis, reflected in the fact that whereas it is located in the Southern African region and is a member of the Southern African Development Community (SADC), its external interests seem to be clearly noticeable in Central Africa, where it has played a direct role in conflict resolution and its engagement with other former Portuguese colonies and Portugal itself (interview with Martin Rupiah, 2010).[1] Further to this is the fact that MPLA and ZANU-PF have no noticeable pre-1980 relations as MPLA was aligned to the Zimbabwe African People's Union (ZAPU) throughout the anti-colonial struggle. Finally, while Angola is currently showing signs of aspirations to ascendancy as a regional power building on its rich oil and diamonds resources, it has recently emerged from a devastating and long civil war that forced it to concentrate more on internal national reconstruction, and Dos Santos has not proved an active foreign policy practitioner like Mugabe or Thabo Mbeki. Dos Santos spends most of his time in Angola and, since coming to power in 1979, has not been vocal when it comes to regional, continental and international affairs. This might partly explain the silence of Angola *vis-à-vis* the Zimbabwe crisis.

With its main focus on the post-war period, this paper examines four key issues that have a bearing in understanding Angola's post-war relationship with Zimbabwe since 2002. It starts off with a brief analysis of the key drivers of Angolan foreign policy in general and the particular evolution of the historical relationship between

ZANU-PF and MPLA since the time of anti-colonial struggles of the 1970s with a view to understanding how these might have shaped the two parties' bilateral relations as well as their relations with the region. It proceeds to piece together aspects of the current foreign policy standpoint between ZANU-PF and MPLA with a particular focus on the Zimbabwe–Angola collaborative military intervention in the Democratic Republic of Congo (DRC) in 1998. The paper also examines the relations between MPLA and the Movement for Democratic Change (MDC) as reflected in the recent state visit by Morgan Tsvangirai (MDC-T President) to Luanda in October 2009. This visit was followed by an announcement by ZANU-PF of China-Sonangol's $8bn investment in November 2009, which also needs to be analysed as part of another dimension in making sense of current MPLA–ZANU-PF relations. Throughout the paper an attempt is made to understand the role Angola has played in the resolution of the post-2000 political and economic instability (both bilaterally and regionally) together with an assessment of any policy implications for the ongoing regional initiative to resolve the Zimbabwe crisis.

Background: Development of Angola's Complex Foreign Policy

Angola has evolved a complex foreign policy since its achievement of political independence in 1975. Its foreign policy has been driven by a combination of historical and ideological considerations on the one hand, and pragmatism linked to challenges of nation-building, problems of economic reconstruction and realities of winning a civil war on the other hand (Ogunbadejo, 1981, pp. 254–269). In the first place, Angolan political independence was achieved largely through the support of the Soviet Union and Cuba, the two godfathers of socialism (Shubin, 2007, pp. 251–262). Inevitably, ideology became a crucial determinant in the direction of the country's foreign policy.

The situation was further complicated by the fact that while MPLA emerged victorious in the liberation struggle and formed the first post-colonial government of Angola, the liberation struggle had involved two other liberation movements, namely the National Front for the Liberation of Angola (FNLA) led by Holden Roberto and the National Union for the Total Independence of Angola (UNITA) under Jonas Savimbi, which were sponsored by the United States and China, respectively (Malaquias, 2000, p. 1). These two movements contested the ascendancy of MPLA to power and this resulted in Angola's decolonisation project quickly degenerating into civil war that ranged on until 2002 following the death of Savimbi. Angola's problems were exacerbated by its imbrications within the complex Cold War politics, which reduced it in the eyes of some observers to a proxy of Soviet and Cuban expansion into Southern Africa (MacFarlane, 1989; Othieno, 2005; Gleijeses, 2006). The Angolan government's offer of rear bases to liberation movements such as ZAPU, South West Africa People's Organisation (SWAPO) and the African National Congress (ANC) within its borders was meant to integrate it to the region and to isolate those forces such as UNITA that were considered as counter-revolutionary formations; but this action of Angola invited apartheid South Africa's intervention through its 'total strategy', which legitimised military raids into Angola, together with sponsorship of UNITA (Friedland, 1981, pp. 95–105; Davies, 1990, pp. 181–190).

Thus, throughout the 1970s right up to the signing of the New York Accord on 22 December 1998, which provided for a period of 27 months for the withdrawal of Cuban forces in return for the withdrawal of South African forces and implementation of the United Nations (UN) plan for the decolonisation of Namibia, Angola has been a host to both friendly and uninvited and hostile actors, which had an impact on the development of its foreign policy. Angola as a young post-colonial African state born in 1975 had to make various hard choices to navigate complex Cold War politics, survive as a state, weather internal war, and avoid degeneration into a failed state at the end of the Cold War. This complexity in Angolan foreign policy was captured well by Oye Ogunbadejo (1981, p. 254) who stated that:

> As time wore on, and as the harsh realities of nation-building persistently stared the MPLA leaders straight in the eye, a good measure of realism was adopted: the once one-lane ideological express-way to Havana and Moscow was broadened and redesigned to have numerous access routes to the West.

Angola was not able to abandon the Soviet Union, which provided it with the bulk of the arms and ammunition with which MPLA used to fight against Portuguese colonialism in the first instance and to survive the combined post-colonial internal onslaught by FNLA and UNITA in the second instance. Cuba participated directly in assisting the MPLA to repel and defeat UNITA and South African Defence Forces (SADF) unleashed on Angola by the apartheid regime. Throughout the 1970s, the United States and China did not support the MPLA, with the Central Intelligence Agency (CIA) of the Unite States aiding the FNLA based in Zaire (now the DRC) and China sponsoring UNITA (Legum & Hodges, 1976; Stockwell, 1978; Marcum, 1978). UNITA–China relations dated back to the time Savimbi underwent military training in China in 1964 and 1965. During the late 1960s, UNITA even masqueraded as a political force guided by Maoist thought. In the face of these realities, Angola under the MPLA had no option but to solidify its linkages with Moscow and Havana, which supported what was considered to be progressive liberation movements, such as the Popular Movement for the Liberation of Angola (MPLA), African National Congress (ANC), South West Africa People's Organisation (SWAPO), Front for the Liberation of Mozambique (FRELIMO) and Zimbabwe African People's Union (ZAPU), rather than splinter ones that were considered to be counter-revolutionary and divisive, such as UNITA and FNLA in Angola, the Zimbabwe African National Union (ZANU, which broke away from ZAPU in 1963) in Zimbabwe and the Pan-Africanist Congress (PAC, which broke away from the ANC in 1959) in South Africa (Howe, 1969, pp. 150–165).

As a result of the MPLA's reliance on Soviet and Cuban assistance, it deeply imbibed Marxist-Leninist ideology. In December 1977 at its first congress, the MPLA chose deliberately to restructure itself into a Marxist-Leninist style party with a Central Committee and Politburo and other Eastern Bloc-oriented organisational structures (*New Africa Magazine*, February 1979). Since then, the MPLA has continued to try and discipline internal elitist-bourgeois tendencies while projecting itself as a political force rooted in workers and peasant classes. Socialism had been chosen as the mechanism through which a Portuguese-crafted colonial economy could be transformed to serve national interests and those of the formerly excluded peasants and workers.

Throughout the 1970s, however, the MPLA was riddled by internal ideological battles, with ideological puritans favouring strict Leftism, the moderates who wanted rapprochement with the West and those who favoured a pragmatic non-aligned foreign policy favourable to solidarity with other national liberation movements in particular and 'Third World' solidarity movements opposed to imperialism and colonialism in general. These battles led to the bloody but abortive coup in May 1977 that witnessed the murder of many the closest collaborators of Agostinho Neto, who was seen as veering too much to the Left. The coup was spearheaded by Nito Alves.[2] The other grievance was that the MPLA was dominated by cadres of mixed blood commonly known as *mesticos* in Angola rather than black Angolans. This led President Neto to increase the number of black Angolans in the Politburo to avert further internal troubles within the MPLA.

By 1979, Neto had discovered the limits of a strictly pro-Soviet foreign policy in solving multi-faceted and deep-rooted economic problems. He began to make overtures to the West, admitting that strict pro-Soviet policies could no longer be maintained in economic relations and policies. Neto emphasised the need for Western aid, technology and investment (Ogunbadejo, 1981, p. 259). Angola also emphasised that its foreign policy was hinged on non-alignment, which was going to liberate MPLA in terms of pursuit of its interests in world affairs; but there was an irony in this foreign policy shift, as well put by Assis Malaquias (2000, p. 4):

> Ironically, Agostinho Neto sought to navigate the turbulent period of the Cold War by adopting a non-aligned foreign policy discourse even if, in practice, the MPLA could not realistically hope to abandon the Soviet embrace without threatening its very survival.

Unfortunately, Neto died in September 1979 without living long enough to implement what he was proposing. He was succeeded by Jose Eduardo dos Santos, a Soviet-trained petroleum engineer. Dos Santos immediately abandoned any pretence towards non-alignment and moved Angola 'closer' to the Soviet Union and Cuba, giving greater space for the Soviet influence in domestic and foreign policy of the country (Malaquias, 2000, p. 5). Inevitably, this increasing closeness of Angola to the Soviets and Cubans in the 1980s provoked the emergence of the 'Reagan Doctrine', which took the form of a global strategy to provide overt support to UNITA as a tool to fight MPLA and replace it as the government of Angola 'either through ballots or bullets' (Malaquias, 2000, p. 5). UNITA received sophisticated US weaponry, including Stinger anti-aircraft missiles that diminished MPLA air supremacy (MacFarlane, 1992; Crocker, 1992). This culminated in the failure of successive MPLA government military offensives against UNITA in the 1980s. A military stalemate emerged that resulted in a search for a negotiated resolution of the Angolan problems.

The Angolan search for a negotiated settlement coincided with the end of the Cold War, which had the effect of diminishing the global patronage and sponsorship that had sustained both UNITA and MPLA as fighting forces (O'Neil and Muslow, 1990, pp. 81–96). Cuba, which had been siding with the MPLA and apartheid South Africa, which had been supporting UNITA, both succumbed to changed post-Cold War international realities and accepted the inevitability of a negotiated settlement.

This change of mindset in some of the actors in the Angolan conflict culminated in the withdrawal of Cuban forces from Angola and implementation of United Nations Security Council Resolution 435/78 regarding Namibia's independence. The withdrawal of 50,000 Cuban forces within a period of 27 months from Angola in return for the implementation of the UN plan for Namibian independence, facilitated by the New York Accord of 22 December 1988, marked the beginning of the resolution of the Angolan conflict (O'Neil and Muslow, 1990, p. 81).

This initiative would remove the South African military threat from Namibia and deny UNITA a vital supply route from the south. The weakness of the New York Accord was that it excluded UNITA as part of the MPLA insistence on the separation of domestic from regional issues. To MPLA, UNITA was now a domestic issue that was to be resolved through either direct negotiations or military solution. MPLA's reluctance to pursue a negotiated solution was indicated by its insistence that UNITA was an illegitimate political force, armed and financed by outside forces, and its unpreparedness to share power with such a force. It would seem MPLA's plan was to isolate UNITA and then defeat it militarily once South African forces had disengaged from Namibia and Angola (Malaquias, 2000, p. 6).

The problem was that MPLA had underestimated UNITA's ability to survive without patrons. Savimbi rejected the resolution of civil war through harmonisation and clemency. UNITA still enjoyed US sponsorship via Zaire; but both the MPLA and UNITA were under pressure to find a political solution to the civil war. The second initiative to solve the Angolan conflict took the form of the Bicesse Peace Accord, signed by both the MPLA and UNITA in May 1991 in Lisbon. This initiative failed and in November 1992, following a failed electoral process, MPLA and UNITA were back at war; but what the Bicesse Accord had succeeded in doing was to mark the elimination of what Malaquias (2000, p. 5) termed 'the proxy war stage of conflict'. Both MPLA and UNITA used mostly local resources (oil and diamonds) to sponsor the round of war after 1992.

I shall return to the Angolan search for peace in the 1990s via what Malaquias (2000, p. 7) termed an 'African solution for Angola's domestic problems' in the next section. It is important now to discuss the development of relations between MPLA and ZANU-PF as Robert Mugabe became active in the resolution of the Angolan crisis in the late 1980s, including hosting a summit of African leaders in Harare on 22 August 1989, and was the first Southern African leader openly to describe Savimbi as an 'international terrorist', thus winning the hearts of the MPLA, which considered UNITA to be a 'terrorist' organisation without political legitimacy.

ZANU-PF and MPLA Relations

Throughout the years of the liberation struggle that culminated in the political independence of Angola in 1975 and the subsequent achievement of political independence by Zimbabwe on 18 April 1980, ZANU-PF–MPLA relations were tenuous rather than cordial. At birth in 1963, as a splinter organisation from ZAPU, ZANU entered a hostile international and regional arena. The ZANU predicament was well captured by William Cyrus Reed, who wrote that:

The external environment which ZANU entered in 1964 was dominated by ZAPU. Regionally, ZAPU and its predecessor the Southern Rhodesia African National Congress, had actively collaborated with Kenneth Kaunda and Hastings Banda to secure the break-up of the European-dominated Central African Federation. Similarly, ZAPU's president, Joshua Nkomo, had been an active participant in the Pan-African Movement of East, Central and Southern Africa (PAFMESCA) ... In 1963 PAFMESCA designated ZAPU as its next major recipient of aid ... Not only had PAFMESCA's former secretary-general already begun to generate international support for ZAPU, but ZAPU subsequently received far more support from the OAU than did ZANU. In addition, while OAU policy called for unity among independence movements, ZAPU refused to recognise ZANU as anything than a 'splinter group without a following' whose only option was 'to return to the fold' and it steadfastly refused to form a common front, as ZANU proposed. (Reed, 1993, pp. 36–37)

ZAPU, alongside the ANC, SWAPO, FRELIMO and MPLA, not only received support and recognition from the Soviet Union and many Eastern Bloc countries, but they also were designated as the 'authentic' national liberation movements by the Organisation of African Unity (OAU), which has now assumed the name African Union (AU). These organisations were also linked through the Afro-Asian People's Solidarity Organisation (AAPSO). Thus by the time ZANU was formed, ZAPU had already become a recognised participant in AAPSO and was receiving its support (Reed, 1993, p. 37).

In 1968, those nationalist organisations that were designated as 'authentic' fighters for independence mounted a major diplomatic initiative to prevent splinter groups such as ZANU from gaining international recognition and support. It was within this context that one can understand why there were no direct linkages between MPLA and ZANU throughout the 1970s. MPLA was a strong ally of ZAPU throughout the time of liberation struggle. After 1975, MPLA offered military training facilities to ZAPU and a number of cadres of the Zimbabwe People's Revolutionary Army (ZIPRA—the military wing of ZAPU) trained in Angola (interview with a Colonel of the Zimbabwean Army, 2010).[3]

Reed noted that ZANU's initial sources of external support came from Tanzania, Ghana and Zambia. While in Zambia ZANU was just tolerated, its ties with Ghana and Tanzania 'stemmed from personal frustration of their respective leaders— Kwame Nkrumah and Julius Nyerere—with ZAPU's president, Joshua Nkomo, and the appeal of ZANU's more confrontational approach' (Reed, 1993, p. 37). Nyerere was further encouraged to support ZANU because of the personal confidence that had developed between him and Herbert Chitepo, who became ZANU's national chairman up until his assassination in 1975 (Republic of Zambia, 1976; Martin and Johnson, 1985). Chitepo had worked in Tanzania as director of public prosecutions. Nkrumah had developed personal ties with Robert Mugabe, who had lived and taught in Ghana and undergone ideological training at Kwame Nkrumah Ideological Institute at Winneba before becoming active in Zimbabwean nationalist politics in the 1960s (Reed, 1993, p. 38).

ZANU also benefited from a break between the Soviet Union and China that took place in the late 1960s. China's search for clients coincided with ZANU's search for patrons (Reed, 1993, p. 40; Ndlovu-Gatsheni, 2009a, p. 315–317). In the late 1960s, ZANU deployed armed men into Rhodesia as part of its efforts to impress international patrons and win recognition by the OAU as an authentic liberation movement worthy of international support. It was in this context that in April 1966 ZANU sent seven armed men into Rhodesia who were annihilated by Rhodesian forces at Sinoia (now Chihnoyi). As argued by Reed (1993, p. 39), 'the battle of Chinoia was a public relations bonanza for ZANU, which now claimed massive support throughout the country'. This rather ill-planned deployment of men by ZANU was quickly popularised as marking the start of the 'Chimurenga War' (Martin and Johnson, 1981); but throughout the liberation struggle until 1976 when ZAPU and ZANU formed an alliance known as the Patriotic Front (PF), the latter still lagged behind the former in competition for international friends.

By 1969, ZANU was still struggling to connect with established liberation movements such as ZAPU, ANC, FRELIMO, SWAPO and MPLA. For instance, at the World Peace Council of 1969 and AAPSO, the Soviet linkages dominated and the established movements were favoured. China then came in and supported the rival groups and the ZANU–China relations were consolidated through ZANU cadres such as Josiah Magama Tongogara and Emmerson Mnangagwa undergoing training in guerrilla warfare at Nanking Academy in Beijing. This was followed by China sending military instructors to train the Zimbabwe National Liberation Army (ZANLA, ZANU's military wing) at Itumbi Training Base in Tanzania in the early 1970s (Martin and Johnson, 1981).

ZANU did not, however, give up approaching established liberation movements for alliances. Its breakthrough came in the early 1970s, when FRELIMO offered it bases in Mozambique. ZANU had capitalised on an internal crisis in ZAPU that made it fail to take up the offer of bases in Mozambique as an old ally of FRELIMO.[4] By 1972, ZANU was enjoying tenuous backing from FRELIMO and it quickly demonstrated its commitment to armed liberation of Zimbabwe through the deployment of ZANLA, who immediately attacked Altena Farm in north-eastern Zimbabwe. In the same year, ZANU issued its radical policy statement known as Mwenge II, where it presented itself as the vanguard of a revolution for socialist transformation. It also divided the world into a retrogressive capitalist/imperialist camp and a progressive socialist camp. It placed the Soviet Union in the retrogressive imperialist camp and China in the progressive socialist camp (Nyangoni and Nyandoro, 1979).

Before his assassination, Chitepo, the Chairman of ZANU's *Dare* (War Council), engaged in serious engagement of the international world in search of allies. In the West ZANU allied itself with any forces that professed a Leftist orientation. Chitepo visited such socialist countries as Romania, Bulgaria and Yugoslavia as well as India, Sweden, New Zealand, Australia and the Netherlands (Reed, 1993, p. 42); but by 1974, ZANU still had not found many useful friends to the extent that it suffered severe shortages of supplies, which provoked internal dissension between the armed wing and the political leadership, leading to the Nhari Rebellion (Bhebe and Ranger, 1995).[5]

The period 1974–75 witnessed not only the internal troubles in ZANU but also the achievement of independence by Mozambique and Angola as well as South

Africa and Rhodesia initiating the policy of detente. Detente was a policy that was aimed at securing a negotiated settlement in Rhodesia supported by the principal regional actors in Southern Africa. The detente initiative provoked the independent African states of Southern Africa (Botswana, Zambia, Mozambique, Angola and Tanzania) to meet and formulate a common front known as the Front Line States (FLS) to make sure they spoke with one voice regarding the decolonisation of remaining of colonies (Thompson, 1986, p. 14). Besides the FLS demanding the unity of all liberation forces fighting for the liberation of Zimbabwe, they also recognised ZANU as a liberation force on condition that it cooperated and united with others into one nationalist movement. MPLA was now the ruling party in Angola and featured in support of the liberation of Zimbabwe through FLS and offering training bases to ZAPU. By 1975, the FLS had forced ZAPU, ZANU, FROLIZI and the African National Council (ANC of Zimbabwe, which was led by Bishop Abel Muzorewa) to unite under ANC. OAU also recognised the expanded ANC.[6]

ZANU also, however, suffered the burden of being forced to accept Reverend Ndabaningi Sithole as its leader, imposed by the OAU and FLS. Sithole had long suffered a 'prison coup'. Even Samora Machel did not entertain the idea of a new ZANU leader other than Sithole. Added to this, the consequences of the assassination of Chitepo were drastic for ZANU (Sithole, 1999).[7] Its offices were closed in Tanzania and Zambia. Mozambique threatened to throw them out too. ZANU lost international recognition. It was partly this crisis that led ZANU to cooperate with ZAPU. First, they accepted the formation of a united military front known as Zimbabwe Independence People' Army (ZIPA), which comprised forces from ZIPRA and ZANLA (Moore, 1995, pp. 73–103). Second, it accepted the formation of the PF as a political alliance with ZAPU (Stedman, 1991).

Not only was PF a blessing to ZANU, but also the FLS accepted Mugabe as the leader of ZANU. On official assumption of ZANU leadership in 1977 at a party conference held at Chimoio in Mozambique, Mugabe not only focused his attention on internal consolidation of ZANU but also embarked on a many trips to generate international support for his party. The trips saw him visiting Ethiopia, Syria, Pakistan, China, Vietnam, North Korea, Cuba, Gabon, Yugoslavia and Sudan between 1978 and 1979 (Reed, 1993 pp. 46–47). At the Lancaster House Conference where the Zimbabwean decolonisation was negotiated, ZANU stuck with ZAPU as part of the PF throughout the negotiations, in the process gaining acceptance by ZAPU allies as well (Stedman, 1991, pp. 110–113). Thus, by the time Zimbabwe achieved independence on 18 April 1980, Mugabe had managed to establish linkages with many countries and ZANU was becoming fully accepted as a legitimate liberation movement.

MPLA and ZANU-PF's Search for Regional Allies

William C. Reed (1993, p. 54) argued that 'the international alliances and animosities ZANU developed during the liberation struggle serve as guideposts for the foreign policy activities which Zimbabwe's ZANU-dominated government has pursued'. This analysis is amplified by Hasu Patel (2006, p. 175), who argued that 'since 1980 there has been an organic link between the method of independence, that is the armed struggle (the Second Chimurenga) for independence, and its values and beliefs, and domestic and foreign policy'.

At the global level, the first country to suffer was the Soviet Union, which had sponsored ZAPU throughout the liberation struggle. As the pre-1980 hostilities between ZANU-PF and PF-ZAPU came to the surface barely two years into the Government of National Unity (GNU) formed in 1980, ZANU-PF suspected that the Soviets would sponsor PF-ZAPU to destabilise Zimbabwe and eventually stage a military take-over of government in Harare. ZANU-PF feared what the Soviets had done in Angola, where they supported MPLA to emerge victorious as the new government in Luanda. This was clearly manifested through ZANU-PF's refusal to permit Moscow to open an embassy in Harare for three years after independence. ZANU-PF also endeared itself to Washington, which emerged as Zimbabwe's largest single donor in the 1980s. This action was taken in spite of ZANU-PF's continued use of Marxist-Leninist rhetoric (Reed, 1993, p. 54).

In the region, ZANU-PF saw the need to integrate itself and form alliances with the African independent states but remained suspicious of movements such as the ANC and ruling parties such as MPLA that had close ties with PF-ZAPU. As such, ZANU-PF decided to build on relationships developed prior to independence, hence its consolidation of ties with Tanzania and Mozambique first. Zimbabwe and Tanzania worked together in sending troops to defend central Mozambique in general and the Beira Corridor in particular from attacks by the rebel movement RENAMO;[8] but ZANU-PF also aimed to isolate PF-ZAPU, which had constituted itself as a major opposition party to ZANU-PF in the 1980s. This it did partly by sending ZANU-PF representatives and former ZANLA elements as military attachés to countries such as Angola. This was done at the expense of former ZIPRA members serving in the Zimbabwe National Army (ZNA), some of whom were trained in Angola (interview with a Colonel of the Zimbabwe National Army, 2010).

ZANU-PF tried also to avoid early development of close ties with the ANC of South Africa because it was an ally of ZAPU dating back to the late 1960s when ZIPRA and Umkonto weSizwe cadres staged combined operations in Rhodesia.[9] Since that time, ZANU claimed to have formed an alliance with PAC and the relations with the ANC were never close until 1987, when PF-ZAPU joined ZANU-PF under the Unity Accord (Ellis and Sechaba, 1992). However, the attempt by ZANU-PF to shun some governments and liberation movements formerly associated with PF-ZAPU did not tally with its professed guidelines of its post-colonial foreign policy. In August 1980, Mugabe outlined five principles guiding Zimbabwe's foreign policy in a speech at the UN. The five principles were as follows:

- national sovereignty and equality among nations;
- attainment of a socialist egalitarian and democratic society;
- right of all peoples to self-determination and independence;
- non-racialism at home and abroad; and
- positive non-alignment and peaceful coexistence among nations (Patel, 1985, pp. 229–230).

As argued by Patel, these principles incorporated ideals of nationalism, Pan-Africanism, anti-imperialism, solidarity, non-intervention and non-interference in internal affairs, multilateralism and the 'Look East Policy', which has become more prominent since the end of the 1990s (Chan and Patel, 2006, p. 176). In line with these principles, Zimbabwe had to support such forces as the MPLA, which was defending its sovereignty, and ANC, which was fighting for self-determination and democratic society, and against non-racialism. These principles guided ZANU-PF's continued search for friends in the region and internationally that began at its formation in 1963. As put by Martin Rupiah:

> After winning the independence elections and after forming the new government, ZANU-PF pursued a deliberate policy of finding friends all over the world. In the region, it wanted to establish linkages with all former liberation movements as part of its strategy to integrate itself within the region in particular and the continent in general. It was in the 1980s that ZANU-PF opened lines of communication with MPLA. ZANU-PF wanted to inherit the sole title of being the sole authentic liberation that fought for the independence of Zimbabwe. This entailed working hard in isolating PF-ZAPU from its former allies as part of safeguarding ZANU-PF's regime security. (Interview with Martin Rupiah, 2010)

Rupiah's analysis of the development of ZANU-PF–MPLA relations was also echoed by a former ZIPRA combatant who is currently serving as a colonel in ZNA who stated that:

> ZANU-PF is treading carefully in its relations with those countries and national movements that were associated and supported ZAPU and ZIPRA during the liberation struggle like Angola. The caution has taken the form of sending non-ex-ZIPRA military attaches to Angola so as to destroy any traces of ZAPU and ZIPRA legacy in the region and internationally. A crusade to erase ZAPU and ZIPRA from the history of liberation began here at home in 1980 and was extended to the region and internationally. (Interview with Colonel of the Zimbabwe National Army, 2010)

Just like Zimbabwe, Angola had, since 1975, premised its foreign policy on 'enfeeblement, if not destruction, of its domestic security threat' (Malaquias, 2000, p. 9). Angola sought to isolate and destroy UNITA in the same manner that ZANU-PF sought to isolate, destroy or swallow PF-ZAPU in the 1980s. By 1999, MPLA had succeeded in isolating UNITA and made friends with Zimbabwe, Namibia, South Africa, the DRC and Congo-Brazzaville. What was left was then to defeat UNITA militarily, and this happened in 2002.

At another level, Mugabe became a vocal advocate of the total decolonisation of Africa and openly condemned the apartheid system in South Africa alongside such movements as UNITA and RENAMO that were destabilising Angola and Mozambique. As an advocate of Pan-Africanism, supporter of principles of self-determination and independence of African states, Zimbabwe: intervened in Mozambique on the side of the FRELIMO government; participated in UN peace-keeping operations in Angola, including assuming the position of UN Force Commander, and in Somalia where it assumed UN Deputy Force Commander position; played a role in mediation in Mozambique and Angola in the period 1989–91; and intervened in the DRC in 1998, assuming overall command of a combined force of Zimbabweans, Angolans and Namibians (Patel, 1993). Through these activities coupled with Mugabe's consistent anti-imperialism and anti-colonial speeches, Zimbabwe won many supporters in the region, continent and the broader South. Throughout the 1980s and early 1990s, Mugabe assumed a status of a consistent revolutionary in many circles who spoke on behalf of the formerly colonised parts of the world. He also emerged as a consistent Pan-Africanist (Phimister and Raftopoulos, 2004, pp. 385–390).

As part of its role in conflict resolution in Africa, on 22 August 1989 Zimbabwe hosted a follow-up Summit of African Heads of State on Angola in Harare as a sequel to the Gbadolite Special Summit of African Heads of States convened by Mobutu Sese Seko on 22 June 1989 in Zaire, at which Dos Santo and Savimbi met for the first time (Malaquias, 2000, p. 7). This was the first initiative moulded along the philosophy of 'African Solutions to African Problems' that Mugabe has continued to parrot up to today. By the time of the Harare Summit, Mugabe had made it clear that in the Angolan conflict he sided with MPLA against UNITA. Savimbi was not even invited to participate, mainly because of Mugabe's open hostility towards UNITA. As noted by Malaquias (2000, p. 7), Mugabe was not in a position or willing to give Savimbi 'the benefit of the doubt as Mobutu had been'. The outcome of the Harare Summit was inevitably a diplomatic triumph for MPLA as it included such a bizarre suggestion as voluntary exile for Savimbi and integration of UNITA into existing MPLA institutions. When Savimbi rejected the plan, Mugabe continued to denounce him. At the same time, MPLA continued to battle UNITA through a combination of military assaults and minor concessions.

The development of mutual trust between Angola and Zimbabwe, however, has clearly been demonstrated in recent years in their collaborative intervention in the DRC alongside Namibia at the invitation of Laurent Kabila. Zimbabwe acted on the basis of the terms of the SADC Organ on Politics, Defence and Security, which was an outgrowth of the old FLS arrangements (Rupiah, 2002, p. 160). Zimbabwe went on to urge for a Defence Pact with Angola, the DRC and Namibia, which South Africa avoided acceding to this body. Martin Rupiah, an academic specialist on defence and security issues in the SADC region, noted that the Defence Pact was concocted during the course of the DRC war and came into effect retrospectively (interview with Martin Rupiah, 2010). South Africa favoured delegating to bureaucrats the security issues under the Organ on Politics, Defence and Security, whereas Zimbabwe was convinced that regional security issues need to be handled at SADC Heads of State level. This divergence of interpretation spoiled relations, particularly between Nelson Mandela and Mugabe, as well as affecting the consolidation of regional security arrangements (Cilliers and Malan, 2001).

Zimbabwe and Angola have strategic interests in the DRC. The giant Inga Dam in the DRC supplied part of Zimbabwe's electricity. To the Angolans, the coming to power of Laurent Kabila in Kinshasa provided a friendly neighbour that was opposed to UNITA, unlike Zaire under Mobutu Sese Seko, which had harboured FNLA and UNITA; but these strategic interests had to be coded and disguised under a combination of preservation of sovereignty of the DRC and SADC commitment to promotion of peace and stability in the region (Chan and Patel,

2006, p. 177).[10] Since Zimbabwe–Angola's collaborative intervention in the DRC, ZANU-PF increasingly supported MPLA against UNITA up until the death of Savimbi in 2002.

On the other hand, Angola has not clearly expressed its foreign policy towards Zimbabwe except for some solidarity statements whenever MPLA officials visited Harare. Gorden Moyo, the Minister of State in the Prime Minister's Office in Harare, stated that Angola has avoided openly expressing its foreign policy towards Zimbabwe and its position *vis-à-vis* the Zimbabwe crisis (interview with Minister of State in the Prime Minister's Office Gorden Moyo, 2010).[11] On the Zimbabwean side, ZANU-PF panicked when the MDC was formed in September 1999 and when it demonstrated its ability to unseat ZANU-PF from power by spearheading a 'no vote' in the Constitutional Referendum of February 2000. ZANU-PF's panic was reflected in its attempts to revive the liberation war-time nationalism and efforts to mobilise the former liberation movements in the region behind it, as it proclaimed that it was fighting a *Third Chimurenga*[12] aimed at rebuffing MDC as a 'running dog of imperialism' in cahoots with latter-day colonialists led by Britain on one front, and engaged in taking decolonisation to its logical conclusion, which was economic empowerment of blacks via fast-track land reform on the other front (Mugabe, 2001; Ndlovu-Gatsheni and Muzondidya, forthcoming, 2011).

In short, the formation of the MDC with clear backing and support from the youth and Western powers ignited another round of competition with ZANU-PF for friends in the region, continent and internationally. This is the context within which MDC–MPLA relations can be understood, as analysed below.

Morgan Tsvangirai's State Visit to Luanda: MDC–MPLA Relations

Since the controversy-ridden 29 March 2008 harmonised parliamentary, senatorial and presidential elections, MDC-T under Morgan Tsvangirai has evolved a regional and continental offensive in search of friends and to explain its political position. Martin Rupiah defined the regional offensive as a combination of SADC and Africa initiative underpinned by four core aims: explaining the MDC-T political position; destroying the idea that MDC-T is a front for re-colonisation of Zimbabwe and a proxy for Western interests; isolating ZANU-PF, which has tried to monopolise the region and the continent as its permanent support base; and trying to overcome the security sector threat of a coup if MDC were to come to power through winning free and fair elections (interview with Martin Rupiah, 2010). This strategy was crafted within a context in which MDC-T emerged a winner in the parliamentary elections and Tsvangirai beat Mugabe in the first round of presidential race, but they were not able to translate this into ascendancy to state power owing to ZANU-PF and the security sector's threat to 'shoot the ballot' and remain in power (Ndlovu-Gatsheni, 2009a).

In the region, Botswana was the first country to embrace MDC-T to the extent of offering Tsvangirai a place of refuge immediately after the March elections. The second country to reveal sympathies with MDC-T was Kenya through Prime Minister Odinga Odinga, who, like Tsvangirai, complained of having been denied outright victory by the incumbent government of Mwai Kibaki. MDC also found solidarity from the South African Congress of Trade Unions (COSATU) and other labour unions in the region.[13] The MDC-T strategy also involved lobbying the UN, AU and SADC to intervene in Zimbabwe. The late Zambian President Levy Mwanawasa, who was the Chairman of SADC when the elections took place in Zimbabwe, was also very critical of the way ZANU-PF and Mugabe were running Zimbabwe and was poised to offer MDC-T a sympathetic ear. Even the AU did not endorse the sham elections of June 2008 where Mugabe ran unopposed when Tsvangirai withdrew from the race citing escalating violence against his supporters.[14] AU and SADC recommended third-party mediation by Thabo Mbeki, by then the president of South Africa.

After protracted negotiations, Mbeki managed to make MDC-T, ZANU-PF and MDC-M sign a Memorandum of Understanding (MOU) and later the Global Political Agreement (GPA) in September 2008, which culminated in the formation of the current Inclusive Government in February 2009. By September 2009, however, a crisis had developed within the Inclusive Government, leading to the withdrawal of MDC-T from participating in cabinet meetings caused by unfulfilled provisions of the GPA and continued harassment of MDC-T supporters. It was during the brief disengagement by the MDC that Tsvangirai embarked on further regional and continental engagements that saw him visiting Zambia, Mozambique, DRC, Angola, Tanzania and Libya. As stated by Minister of State in the Prime Minister's Office Gorden Moyo, this round of trips was to engage ZANU-PF's former allies and Mugabe's contemporaries as part of further attempts to isolate ZANU-PF and Mugabe (interview with Minister of State in the Prime Minister's Office Gorden Moyo, 2010). Martin Rupiah added that the other aim was to open direct lines of communication between the Prime Minister's Office and the region as well as the rest of Africa. MDC-T also sought to engage middle-powers of Asia, Latin America and China. To Rupiah, Zimbabwe has no coordinated foreign policy at the moment besides the ZANU-PF fraction of the Inclusive Government's insistence on its old 'Look East Policy' and emerging MDC-T foreign policy founded on re-engagement of Western democracies as well as the rest of the world (interview with Martin Rupiah, 2010).

In terms of how MDC-T went about organising the Prime Minister's visit to the regional capitals in October 2009, Martin Rupiah explained that he played a pivotal role that consisted of three phases. The first phase included contacting the heads of the intelligence service of the selected countries with whom he discussed the intention of the Prime Minister to visit. The second phase involved sending an advance team from MDC-T that opened the lines of communication with members of the intelligence, the military and government and tested the levels of MDC-T's welcome. The final phase then involved the 'state visit' by the Prime Minister (interview with Martin Rupiah, 2010). Rupiah said that even MDC-T was surprised by the 'fertile ground' they found at both party and government levels in all the countries they visited, including Angola. In all the countries they visited together with Morgan Tsvangirai, they were received with 'full military honours befitting any head of government'. In Angola they were taken to the Presidential Palace to meet President Dos Santos (interview with Martin Rupiah, 2010). According to Rupiah:

> MDC-T initiatives are succeeding in destroying ZANU-PF monopolisation of the region and the continent as well as appropriation of liberation war history.

These activities were taking place within a context in which political formations in the region, continent and globally are quickly and deliberately forgetting certain aspects of the past rooted in antiquated ideologies like Marxism and Socialism. Countries like China and Angola are fast embracing capitalism. Everything MDC-T is doing is part of work-in-process including exchanging security briefs within the region and the continent. MDC-T is engaging the world at party and government levels and is consolidating ties with labour movements across the region, continent and globally. (Interview with Martin Rupiah, 2010)

While Rupiah was very optimistic on the prospects of further development of MDC–MPLA relations since Tsvangirai's visit in October 2009, the Minister of State in the Prime Minister's Office remained suspicious of Angola's intentions. In the first place, he alluded to the fact that a Chinese ship carrying weapons destined to Zimbabwe in 2008, which was refused permission to dock in the SADC region, 'finally offloaded its deadly weapons' in Angola and they were carried by Angolan Airways into Zimbabwe secretly (interview with Minister of State in the Prime Minister's Office Gorden Moyo, 2010; Fitz, 2009). This action, according to Minister Moyo, indicated that MPLA was supporting the ZANU-PF hardliners and the security sector, which was violating human rights on an unprecedented scale in the aftermath of the 29 March 2008 elections. In the second instance, he said that 'they have it on good record' that some members of Angola forces were part of the Presidential Guard in Zimbabwe. Third, Minister Moyo pointed out that the very week that Tsvangirai visited Luanda, MPLA dispatched its Secretary General to Zimbabwe on an unknown mission to the MDC. What sparked MDC-T suspicions is that the MPLA Secretary General only engaged with ZANU-PF secretly and left the country. Moyo added that:

I suspect the mission of the MPLA Secretary-General to Zimbabwe was to assure ZANU-PF and allay fears about the Prime Minister's visit that it did not amount to MPLA ditching ZANU-PF as an ally. Indeed the undisclosed purpose of the MPLA Secretary-General's visit raises suspicions in the context of coinciding with the PM's visit to Angola. (Interview with Minister of State in the Prime Minister's Office Gorden Moyo, 2010)

ZANU-PF tried to trivialise the visit of Tsvangirai to the regional capitals. The *Herald* newspaper (4 November 2009) even alleged that the MDC leader was just given a very short time to present his case in Mozambique, Angola, Zambia and DRC. This behaviour on the part of ZANU-PF and its media was meant to bolster the view that the SADC region was behind ZANU-PF and Mugabe. This provoked the Prime Minister's Office to put pictures of the visits in the *Prime Minister's Newsletter* demonstrating how red carpets were unrolled for Tsvangirai and how he was welcomed into presidential palaces in Angola, Mozambique and the DRC in particular.

Minister Moyo characterised Angola's relations with Zimbabwe as largely 'asymmetrical' with a leaning towards ZANU-PF. He added, however, that since Morgan Tsvangirai's visit, two more MDC-T delegations had visited Luanda, including the MDC-T Secretary General Tendai Biti, who is also the Minister of

Finance, to explore party-to-party relations further (interview with Minister of State in the Prime Minister's Office, 2010).

During Tsvangirai's visit to Luanda, Dos Santos is said to have encouraged MDC-T to work together with ZANU-PF to implement the GPA to the letter. He also shared with the Zimbabwean Prime Minister the experience of how Angola finally solved the long-standing internal crisis and how MPLA and UNITA were now able to work together (interview with Martin Rupiah, 2010).

Minister Gorden Moyo emphasised that MDC-T and ZANU-PF are currently engaged in fierce competition for friends, space and opinion in the region, continent and across the globe. He added that the welcome with which the MDC-T leader was received in Luanda 'terrified ZANU-PF which has always behaved as if they owned the SADC region' (interview with Minister of State in the Prime Minister's Office Gorden Moyo, 2010). ZANU-PF had to send Emmerson Mnangagwa (Minister of Defence) on a mission that Moyo suspected was meant to tell the Angolans that ZANU-PF was still in control in Harare and to counter the regional initiatives of MDC-T (interview with Minister of State in the Prime Minister's Office Gorden Moyo, 2010). The other area of competition between MDC-T and ZANU-PF is over sourcing of investment funding and international aid. Soon after Tsvangirai's visit to Angola, ZANU-PF announced that it had signed $8bn investment deals in November 2009 with Sonangol, an Angolan company under the control of the political and military elite as well as Chinese.

A Triple Nexus? China, Angola and Zimbabwe

Contemporary Angola–Zimbabwe relations are imbricated in the broader Sino-Africa policy where Angola has, since 2002, emerged as a major recipient of Chinese investment and loans (Chan, 1985, pp. 376–384; Alves, 2010). On this reality, Ana Cristina Alves wrote that:

> From Beijing's perspective, Angola has been one of its most successful and least troublesome partners in the region. Because of its stability and significant oil reserves, Angola has been one of the major African beneficiaries of China's financial largesse. In fact, this feature of the relationship has helped to establish the pattern of resource collateralised loans that has become one of the most distinctive characteristics of Beijing's engagement with Africa in the present decade. (Alves, 2010, p. 178)

On the other hand, ZANU-PF has, since 1992, added an economic thrust to its foreign policy predicated on a 'Look East Policy'. This policy shift was based on an anticipation of future trade, investments, joint ventures, and tourists coming from the East. In the East, China was emerging as a global power able to counter Western and American economic and political hegemony. Zimbabwe also sought to establish links with countries such as Malaysia, India, Pakistan, Singapore, Indonesia, Thailand and Iran (Chan and Patel 2006, p. 178). The Zimbabwe 'Look East Policy' occupied the centre stage of ZANU-PF during the 2000s, as when Zimbabwe suffered international isolation including suspension from the Commonwealth owing to its poor human rights record and failure to adhere to global standards of 'good governance' (Ndlovu-Gatsheni, 2009b, pp. 1139–1158). The 'Look East Policy' coincided with the development of Sino-Africa policy propelled through the 'Going Out' Chinese economic philosophy that focused on increasing Chinese business activity in Africa (Alves, 2010, pp. 10–11).

Having squandered a number of other foreign policy options through peddling nationalist-inspired belligerence and arrogance, particularly against the West and United States, founded on the illusion of 'going it alone', Zimbabwe had no option other than to try and 'Look East'. To some commentators, Zimbabwe's adoption of a 'Look East Policy' reflected nothing other than desperation. For instance, Stephen Chan thought Zimbabwe's foreign policy at the beginning of 2000 hinged on nostalgia: 'The Zimbabwean government is looking backwards, to a bygone Chinese era, to a bygone set of non-aligned principles, to a bygone era when John Major led Britain— this is a pattern of looking backwards and a bankruptcy of new ideas' (Chan and Patel, 2006, p. 181); but Zimbabwe hoped to build on liberation war Sino–ZANU relations to make China their global patron with veto powers at the United Nations Security Council. Zimbabwe also saw China as poised to dominate the world in the 21st century. China has indeed played the role of Zimbabwe's protector at the UN, vetoing the United States and British drive to impose UN sanctions on the country in exchange for gaining inroads into various sectors of Zimbabwe's economy.

What Zimbabwe did not understand was that the Sino-Africa policy was no longer driven by ideology or sympathy with former African liberation movements. As put by Arthur Mutambara (Zimbabwe's Deputy Prime Minister) after his recent visit to Beijing:

> Beijing now sees Zimbabwe only as a business partner not as a friend. China would not give any more loans until Zimbabwe paid back what it already owed ... The Chinese said we'll not condemn you publicly, but we we'll not give you cash, unless we do the right thing, the Chinese will not work with us. (*Mail & Guardian*, 12–18 March 2010, p. 4)

Mutambara's observations seem to confirm Stephen Chan's critique of the prospects of Zimbabwe's 'Look East Policy' premised on antiquated liberation war camaraderie and on expired leftist ideological affinities; but Zimbabwe seems to believe in the idea that the Chinese 'Going Out' policy is different from Western and American economic and political outreach into Africa, which ZANU-PF consistently reduced to imperialism and colonialism in disguise. They see Chinese economic outreach and assistance as premised on benefiting both the lender and the borrower, 'fitting into the win–win cooperation and mutual benefit models that Beijing employs' (Alves, 2010, p. 18). Angola is cited as a good example of this mutual and beneficial linkage with Beijing.

Zimbabwe, since 1992, has increasingly become a destination for cheap Chinese textiles and other goods that are distinguishable by poor quality to the extent of earning a derogative name—'Zhing-Zhong' (Moyo, 2010). Large Chinese corporations have made inroads into key Zimbabwean industries. Other examples include China's Sino-steel, which owns 92% of Zimbabwe's largest ferrochrome producer, ZIMASCO, and Sino-cement, which has emerged as the largest cement factory in Zimbabwe. The latest child on the block is China-Sonangol, which has been awarded various contracts ranging from housing to mining. Sonangol is an Angolan company that has been active in Angola since the end of the civil war. President Dos Santos of Angola has deep and major business interests in Sonangol and controls much of its activities, working together with the Chinese and some Angolan business and political elites (Chabal, 2007, p. 7). Among key stakeholders in Sonangol are members of Chinese Intelligence working closely with members of the Angolan Presidency (Alves, 2010, p. 18).

China-Sonangol is the company that was reported in the ZANU-PF aligned *Herald* news paper in November 2009 to have signed five agreements with Zimbabwe's government. In Zimbabwe, China-Sonangol was described as a private joint venture with Angola's state oil firm. The agreements signed were said to have targeted gold and platinum refining, oil and gas exploration, fuel purchase and distribution, as well as construction of houses and roads. Misheck Sibanda, the Chief Secretary in President Mugabe's office, and the controversial Governor of the Reserve Bank, Gideon Gono, were quick to hail the signing of the investment deal as 'bearing testimony to the relevance and efficacy of the Look East Policy' and continued Chinese support for Zimbabwe (Presse, n.d.). Gono added that 'This deal represents the most significant inward investment inflow in Zimbabwe. This comes at a time when the country is being ridiculed left, right and centre' (Presse, n.d.).

It is, however, important to understand the political context within which this so-called China-Sonangol $8bn investment was announced in November 2009 by ZANU-PF. In the first place, it was announced soon after Tsvangirai's visit to Angola in October 2009. It was announced as part of the achievements of Minister Emmerson Mnangagwa's trip to Angola and China, which followed after Tsvangirai had visited the Western capitals and the United States to seek investment. In the second place, it was announced as part of ZANU-PF rather than Inclusive Government efforts to lure investors into Zimbabwe. MDC political formations were not part of the deal. The Minister of State in the Prime Minister's Office stated that they read about China-Sonangol investment deal in the state-owned *Herald* newspaper, that the Minister of Finance Tendai Biti did not know about it, and that they learnt that the deal was announced by the Minister of Defence, Emmerson Mnangagwa. Moyo suspected that the announcement was nothing but part of ZANU-PF attempts to counter MDC-T's efforts in opening lines of engagement with the West and America and part of Mugabe's agenda to demonstrate the feasibility of the 'Look East Policy'. According to Moyo, ZANU-PF and the hardliners have been trying to prove that Tsvangirai's attempts to re-engage the West and United States did not bring anything in terms of investment and financial aid to Zimbabwe (interview with the Minister of State in the Prime Minister's Office Gorden Moyo, 2010).

Martin Rupiah also dismissed the China-Sonangol $8bn investment deal as part of mere politicking on the part of ZANU-PF. He noted that ZANU-PF wanted to copy MPLA strategy whereby when the IMF and the World Bank refused to extend lines of credit to Angola, they simply turned east and secured loans from the Chinese International Fund (CIF) to finance reconstruction. According to Rupiah, this strategy cannot work for Zimbabwe because by the time the Inclusive Government assumed office, the Chinese had 'imposed sanctions on Zimbabwe without openly stating so. They had disengaged from Zimbabwe' (interview with Martin Rupiah,

2010). Rupiah emphasised that Chinese, like all investors and capitalists, needed profits not mere friendship and wanted their loans to be serviced. Zimbabwe could not service its loans and its politics did not favour business. He concluded that a deal might have been secured but it has not been implemented as the Chinese want Zimbabwe to create an environment conducive for business operations (interview with Martin Rupiah, 2010).

During the long decade of the Zimbabwe crisis, however, the Chinese continued to supply arms and ammunition to Zimbabwe. In the context of arms embargo imposed by Britain, the Zimbabwean military turned to China and bought fighter jets and other arms. The Chinese ship that was refused permission to dock in South Africa and other SADC countries in 2008, which was carrying arms and ammunition destined to Zimbabwe, clearly demonstrated China's continued supply of arms to Zimbabwe. The latest aspect of Zimbabwe–China relations was the choice of President Mugabe to celebrate his 86th birthday at the Chinese embassy in Harare in February 2010. This can be interpreted as a symbolic gesture by Mugabe to demonstrate to the world that the Chinese are his closest friends, and show the West and America that he is not isolated.[15]

Conclusion

In the light of opacity of Angola–Zimbabwe relations, it is not easy to draw clear policy implications of these relations for the resolution of the economic and political crisis in Zimbabwe and for the regional initiative to resolve the Zimbabwe crisis. What is beyond doubt is that while during the time of the liberation struggle ZANU and MPLA did not develop close ties, on ascension to power in 1980, ZANU-PF made deliberate efforts to work closely with liberation movements and independents states in the region. It was not easy for ZANU-PF to develop quickly close ties with MPLA because of the latter's liberation war-time closeness and support for ZAPU. MPLA and ZANU relations were further complicated by the fact that the former was sponsored by the Soviets whereas the latter was supported by the Chinese. During the liberation war in Southern Africa, the Sino-Soviet tension played a role in preventing some liberation movements from developing close ties beyond convergence at the OAU Liberation Committee level. Throughout the time of the liberation struggle, ZANU as a splinter faction of ZAPU had to contend with politics of rejection as an authentic liberation movement as it was born into a world where ZAPU had already established links with MPLA, FRELIMO, ANC and SWAPO, which were considered at the OAU level to be the authentic liberation movements in Southern Africa.

This means that MPLA–ZANU-PF did not develop strong pre-1980 party-to-party relations compared with ZAPU–ANC and ZAPU–MPLA; but as noted by William C. Reed:

Since its independence in 1980, Zimbabwe has emerged as one of the principal forces in African international relations. Harare, the capital, has emerged as a major diplomatic centre and Zimbabwe has served in major leadership position, both at the United Nations, where, only two years after independence it was unanimously elected to the Security Council, and in the Non-Aligned

Movement, which Zimbabwe was selected to chair in 1986. In this capacity, and as a member of the Commonwealth, Zimbabwe actively participated in the decolonisation of Namibia and has actively lobbied the International community for comprehensive sanctions against South Africa. (Reed, 1993, p. 31)

This active Zimbabwean foreign policy under ZANU-PF built on the experiences of the prosecution of mass-based armed liberation that had involved lobbying the international community enabled ZANU-PF to attract new friends and to be seen as a friend of all those people engaged in struggle for political independence, national self-determination and against racism. ZANU-PF deliberately presented itself as a vocal ally of all those fighting in defence of national sovereignty and those still fighting for political independence in Namibia and South Africa.

Since 1975, Angola had been fighting a bitter civil war and the MPLA was active in the politics of isolating its internal enemies FNLA and UNITA. This thrust of foreign policy coincided with that of ZANU-PF in the 1980s, which was also fighting to isolate PF-ZAPU, which was said to be sponsoring 'dissidents'. President Mugabe won the heart of MPLA through his consistent criticism of 'rebel' movements such as UNITA and RENAMO in the SADC region; but it not is clear how MPLA–ZANU-PF relations actually developed in the 1980s beyond activities at the FLS and later SADC level. What is clear is that by 1998 MPLA and ZANU-PF had developed mutual trust to the extent of collaborating in military intervention in the DRC that culminated in the signing of a Defence Pact that Zimbabwe sold to the whole SADC region. Since this collaborative intervention in the DRC, civil society and opposition forces in Zimbabwe have suspected that ZANU-PF and MPLA have exchanged security information and supported each other's regimes. There is a strong belief within the MDC and civil society organisations that the Chinese ship that was carrying arms and ammunition destined for Harare was finally allowed dock in Luanda and the arms were then carried on Angolan Airlines to Harare. To the civil society and opposition forces, this action of Angola indicated its collaboration with the ZANU-PF regime rather than its sympathy with those forces fighting for democracy. The latest manifestation of this collaboration was the China-Sonangol $8bn investment deal that was announced after the Minister of Defence, Emerson Mnangagwa (a ZANU-PF stalwart), visited Luanda and Beijing in November 2009.

Angola has, however, continued to play an unclearly defined role within the SADC without openly expressing its foreign policy thrust *vis-à-vis* the Zimbabwe crisis. This has created more suspicions and speculation. Even the visit by MDC-T leader Morgan Tsvangirai to Luanda in October 2009 has not completely destroyed the suspicions and speculation that MPLA is pro-ZANU-PF rather that pro those forces fighting for democracy in Zimbabwe. If the welcome of MDC-T in Luanda indicates anything, it is that the MPLA government is according both ZANU-PF and MDC lines of communication, while maintaining 'quiet diplomacy' *vis-à-vis* the resolution of the Zimbabwe crisis.

What needs to be added is that Angola, as an emerging regional power and a close ally of China in the SADC region, has some leverage to put pressure on Zimbabwe to implement the GPA. If it can take an open approach to rein in those members of government who are delaying the implementation of the GPA and work closely with South Africa in pushing for an end to the Zimbabwe crisis, as an aspiring regional power it can gain from being seen to be openly supporting democracy. On the other hand, Angola must also be seen to be acting in concert with other SADC states in resisting the so-called 'imperialist sanctions' imposed on Zimbabwe. However, MDC-T is adamant that there are no sanctions imposed on Zimbabwe, there are only restrictive measures targeting those individuals who engaged in acts of violence and violated widespread human rights—but there seem to be consensus in the region that sanctions must be removed.

Notes

1. Interview with retired Lieutenant-Colonel (Dr) Martin Revai Rupiah, Munhumutapa Government Buildings, Harare, Zimbabwe, 11 March 2010. Dr Martin Rupiah is not only a former soldier but also an accomplished academic on issues of security, defence and international affairs. He is now working as a Principal Director within the Prime Minister's Office responsible for international affairs.
2. Besides ideological schisms prompting the bloody abortive coup in May 1977, there were also racial issues. President Neto was being criticised for failing to defend the Angolan working class because his wife was white, his children were of mixed blood (mesticos). MPLA was said to be dominated and led by cadres of mixed blood rather than black Angolans.
3. Interview with a Colonel in the Zimbabwe National Army, 13 March 2010. This colonel, who chose to remain anonymous, is a former ZIPRA combatant, which was a military wing of ZAPU that was given bases during the liberation struggle in Angola.
4. When ZANU initially approached FRELIMO to request access to its territory, FRELIMO replied that it remained allied with ZAPU and offered to cooperate with it rather than ZANU; but by the early 1970s, ZAPU was suffering a second major split that affected its external wing in Zambia. James Chikerema and George Nyandoro, as leaders of ZAPU, were fighting with Jason Ziyapapa Moyo, George Silundika and Edward Ndlovu. The in-fighting was so terrible that it led Chikerema for form a splinter political formation known as the Front for the Liberation of Zimbabwe (FROLIZI).
5. ZANU was suffering the consequences of the assassination of Chitepo, which led the Zambian government to arrest the top leadership of ZANU. By this time, ZANU had no recognised leader. Reverend Ndabaningi Sithole, the founder President of ZANU, had suffered a 'prison coup' and was no longer recognised as the legitimate leader of ZANU by people such as Enos Nkala, Robert Mugabe, Edgar Tekere and Maurice Nyagumbo; but the Front Line States took time to recognise Mugabe as the ZANU leader.
6. FROLIZI and ANC were new additions to the ranks of Zimbabwean liberation movement. They drew members across ZAPU and ZANU divisions. They claimed to be standing for unity among nationalists.
7. The top leadership of ZANU was accused of having taken part in the assassination the party's national chairman due to tribal bickering. Chitepo belonged to the Manyika tribe, which was eliminated by the Karanga tribe.
8. The Beira Corridor was a strategic oil route to Zimbabwe.
9. Between 1967 and 1968, ZAPU in alliance with the ANC sent 150 heavily armed troops into the Wankie Game Reserve and into Sipolilo and Mana Pools in Rhodesia.
10. Stephen Chan disagreed with Hasu Patel on the reasons for Zimbabwe's intervention in the DRC. Chan stated that Patel was wrong in characterising the intervention of Zimbabwe as a contribution to the defence of the DRC against Ugandan and Rwandan invasion. He argued that Zimbabwe's intervention was motivated by interests in mineral deposits that Mugabe used to buy the support of senior military leaders.
11. Interview with Honourable Minister Gorden Moyo, Meikles Hotel, Harare, Zimbabwe, 11 March 2010.
12. *Chimurenga* is a Shona word that is used by ZANU-PF to refer to nationalist liberation struggle against colonialism. Zimbabwe is said to have fought two 'Chimurengas', one in the period 1896–97 and the other in the 1970s.

13. This was mainly because the original MDC emerged from civil society and mainly from the Zimbabwe Congress of Trade Unions; Tsvangirai was its Secretary General.
14. Tsvangirai had to take refuge at the Embassy of the Netherlands in fear of his life. Indeed, ZANU-PF in alliance with war veterans and armed forces were running amok torturing, maiming, raping and killing MDC supporters throughout the country.
15. This was the first time in Mugabe's 30-year rule that he entered a foreign mission, said the Zimbabwe Minister of Foreign Affairs, Simbarashe Mumbengegwi.

References

Alves, A. C. (2010) The oil factor in Sino-Angolan relations at the start of the 21st century, SAIIA Occasional Paper No. 55, February.

Bhebe, N. and Ranger, T. (1995) *Soldiers in Zimbabwe's Liberation War* (Harare: University of Zimbabwe Publications).

Chabal, P. (2007) Introduction: E Pluribus Unum: transitions in Angola, in P. Chabal and N. Vidal (Eds), *Angola: The Weight of History* (London: Hurst), pp. 1–21.

Chan, S. (1985) China's foreign policy and Africa: the rise and fall of China's Three World Theory, *The Round Table*, 382, pp. 376–384.

Chan, S. and Patel, H. (2006) Zimbabwe's foreign policy: a conversation, *The Round Table*, 95(384), pp. 175–190.

Cilliers, J. and Malan, M. (2001) SADC organ on politics, defence and security: future development, 1, 4 and 5, http://www.idsa-india.org/an-may-3.html, accessed 7 April 2009.

Crocker, C. (1992) *High Noon in Southern Africa: Making Peace in a Rough Neighbourhood* (New York: W. Norton).

Davies, R. (1990) South African regional policy before and after Cuito Cuanavale, in G. Moss and I. Obert (Eds), *South Africa Contemporary Analysis* (London: Hans Bell), pp. 181–190.

Ellis, S. and Sechaba, T. (1992) *Comrades against Apartheid: The ANC and the South African Communist Party in Exile* (Bloomington, IN and London: Indiana University Press and James Currey).

Fitz, N. (2009) People power: how civil society blocked an arms shipment for Zimbabwe, SAIIA Occasional Paper No. 36, July.

Friedland, E. A. (1981) South Africa and instability in Southern Africa, *Annals of American Academy of Political and Social Science*, 457, pp. 95–105.

Friedrich-Ebert-Stiftung (2004) The 'Look East Policy' of Zimbabwe now focuses on China, Policy Briefing Paper, Harare, November.

Gleijeses, P. (2006) Moscow's proxy? Cuba and Africa, 1975–1988, *Journal of Cold War Studies*, 8(2), pp. 3–51.

Howe, R. W. (1969) War in Southern Africa, *Foreign Affairs*, 48(1), pp. 150–165.

Legum, C. and Hodges, T. (1976) *After Angola: The War over Southern Africa* (London: Rex Collings).

MacFarlane, S. N. (1989) The Soviet Union and Southern African security, *Problems of Communism*, 38(2–3), pp. 89–102.

MacFarlane, S. N. (1992) Soviet–Angolan relations, 1975–90, in G. W. Bresleuer (Ed.), *Soviet Policy in Africa* (Berkeley: University of California Press).

Malaquias, A. (2000) Angola's foreign policy since independence: the search for domestic security, *Africa Security Review*, 9(3), http://www.iss.co.za/pub/asr/9no3/Angola.html, accessed 17 May 2009.

Marcum, J. A. (1978) *The Angolan Revolution: Volume II: Exile Politics and Guerrilla Warfare, 1962–1976* (Cambridge: MIT).

Martin, D. and Johnson, P. (1981) *The Struggle for Zimbabwe: The Chimurenga War* (Harare: Zimbabwe Publishing House).

Martin, D. and Johnson, P. (1985) *The Chitepo Assassination* (Harare: Zimbabwe Publishing House).

Moore, D. B. (1995) The Zimbabwe people's army: Strategic innovation or more of the same?, in N. Bhebe and T. Ranger (Eds), *Soldiers in Zimbabwe's Liberation War* (London: James Currey), pp. 73–103.

Moyo, J. (2010) Trail of debt all the way to China, *Mail & Guardian*, 12–18 March, p. 9.

Mugabe, R. G. (2001) *Inside the Third Chimurenga: Land is Our Prosperity* (Harare: Government Printers).

Ndlovu-Gatsheni, S. J. (2009a) *Do 'Zimbabweans' Exist? Trajectories of Nationalism, National Identity Formation and Crisis in a Postcolonial State* (Oxford and Bern: Peter Lang AG International Academic Publishers).

Ndlovu-Gatsheni, S. J. (2009b) Making sense of Mugabeism in local and global politics: 'so Blair, keep your England and let me keep my Zimbabwe', *Third World Quarterly*, 30(6), pp. 1139–1158.

Ndlovu-Gatsheni, S. J. and Muzondidya, J. (Eds) (forthcoming, 2011) *Redemptive or Grotesque Nationalism? Rethinking Contemporary Politics in Zimbabwe* (Oxford and Bern: Peter Lang AG International Academic Publishers).

Nyangoni, W. and Nyandoro, G. (1979) *Zimbabwe Independence Movements: Selected Documents* (London: Rex Collings).

Ogunbadejo, O. (1981) Angola: ideology and pragmatism in foreign policy, *International Affairs*, 57(2), pp. 254–269.

O'Neil, K. and Muslow, B. (1990) Ending the Cold War in Southern Africa, *Third World Quarterly*, 12(3), pp. 81–96.

Othieno, T. (2005) Cuba's foreign policy in Angola, *UNISA Latin American Report*, 21(2), pp. 1–10.

Patel, H. (1985) No master, no mortgage, no sale, in T. Shaw and Y. Tandon (Eds), *Regional Development at the International Level: Volume II: African and Canadian Perspectives* (Lanham, MD: University Press of America), pp. 229–230.

Patel, H. (1993) Zimbabwe's mediation in Angola and Mozambique, in S. Chan and V. Jabri (Eds), *Mediation in Southern Africa* (Basingstoke: Macmillan).

Patel, H. (2006) Zimbabwe's foreign policy: a conversation, *The Round Table*, 95(384), pp. 175–190.

Phimister, I. and Raftopoulos, B. (2004) Mugabe, Mbeki and the politics of anti-imperialism, *Review of African Political Economy*, 101, pp. 385–390.

Presse, A. F. (n.d.) Zimbabwe and China ink deal, www.capitalfm.co.ke/newsPrint.php?newsID=6569, accessed 7 April 2009.

Reed, W. C. (1993) International politics and national liberation: ZANU and the politics of contested sovereignty in Zimbabwe, *African Studies Review*, 36(2), pp. 36–37.

Republic of Zambia (1976) Report of the Special Commission on the Assassination of Herbert Wiltshire Chitepo, Lusaka, Zambia.

Rupiah, M. R. (2002) Eight years of tension, misperception and dependence from April 1994 to December 2002 Zimbabwe–South Africa foreign relations: a Zimbabwean perspective, *Alternatives: Turkish Journal of International Affairs*, 1(4), pp. 153–170.

Shubin, V. (2007) Unsung heroes: the Soviet military and the liberation of Southern Africa, *Cold War History*, 7(2), pp. 251–262.

Sithole, M. (1999) *Zimbabwe: Struggles Within the Struggle* (Harare: Rujeko).

Stedman, S. (1991) *Peacemaking in Civil War: International Mediation in Zimbabwe, 1974–1980* (Boulder, CO: Westview Press).

Stockwell, J. (1978) *In Search of Enemies: A CIA Story* (New York: Norton).

Thompson, C. (1986) *Challenge to Imperialism: The Front Line States in the Liberation of Zimbabwe* (Boulder, CO: Westview Press).

Emergence of a New Political Movement

FAY CHUNG

Women's University in Africa, Association for Strengthening Higher Education in Africa, South Africa

Introduction: Background to the 2008 Elections

Zimbabwean politics has tended to be polarised, both before and after independence. Before independence, it was the liberation movement, represented by the Zimbabwe African National Union (ZANU) and the Zimbabwe African People's Union (ZAPU),[1] against the settler-colonial regime, whose final representative was the Rhodesian Front led by Ian Smith. Issues were analysed in an over-simplistic and dogmatic manner: from the side of the liberation forces, you were either 'for liberation' or you were a 'rebel' or a 'sell-out'; from the point of view of the Rhodesian Front, you were either a 'loyal Rhodesian' or you were a 'terrorist', a 'Kaffir lover' and a 'Communist'. 'Rebels', 'sell-outs', 'terrorists', 'Kaffir lovers' and 'Communists' all faced torture, long periods of imprisonment, and possibly the death sentence. These over-simplified and ethnically orientated analyses remain institutionalised in modern day political expression and formations in Zimbabwe. Today, the Zimbabwe African National Union–Patriotic Front (ZANU-PF) demonises all its critics as 'sell-outs' and 'agents of imperialism', whereas the Movement for Democratic Change (MDC) characterises ZANU-PF leaders as 'anti-democratic' and 'corrupt'. President Robert Mugabe is termed a 'dictator' in this war of words. In the midst of this vituperation, there is little room for rational analysis or actual discussion of issues. Both sides appeal to strong emotions. Both sides are weak on detailed analysis of realities, whether political or socio-economic.

In terms of ideological orientation, ZANU-PF managed to transform itself from a 'Marxist–Leninist' party in the 1970s and 1980s to a new 'ideology' based on structural adjustment in the 1990s. 'Structural adjustment' was perceived as a move away from 'socialism' towards 'capitalism', as an influential group within the ZANU-PF leadership, led by then Finance Minister Bernard Chidzero, became convinced that only 'capitalism' could bring about the economic growth that was needed to cope with the needs of the growing population.

Both 'socialism' and 'capitalism' were not clearly defined in any detail by ZANU-PF: the result is that there were varied and even confused explanations of these ideologies. Free primary education and health care were defined as 'socialist', so the introduction of structural adjustment in the 1990s was accompanied by a 'cost recovery' programme for primary education and health care, leading to a drop in primary school enrolments and in the percentage of pregnant women who could access professional assistance at childbirth. The result was an almost threefold increase in maternal mortality.[2] Despite making this tremendous ideological leap within a very short space of time, ZANU-PF's rhetoric and propaganda remained populist, according to the shifting sands of popular demands.

The MDC also had an ideological shift, from the anti-structural adjustment of its trade union base, to pro-neo-liberalism, a shift from one extreme to its opposite. It also appealed to populism, and was able to accommodate the requirements of the trade union movement, while at the same time satisfying the needs of the white landowners. MDC policies comfortably reflected a mixture of social democratic values popular with their worker support and their overseas trade union partners, as well as the demands made on them by their early financial supporters, mainly the white commercial farmers. Policy and strategy documents thus reflected both a left-orientated rhetoric aimed at appealing to the urban workers, and the neo-liberal economics demanded by landowners, multilateral and Western donors.

In terms of economic policies, both ZANU-PF and the MDC today support some version of the Washington consensus. The difference between the two parties is thus not specifically ideological. However, ZANU-PF policies and strategies are aimed at retaining their traditional support from the rural peasants who had supported ZANU throughout the armed struggle. For the rural community, one of the main issues was the shortage of land. Sixty-eight per cent of the population live in rural areas, so if ZANU-PF could manage to retain its hold of the rural areas it would retain its electoral dominance, if not its intellectual and emotional hegemony. The land resettlement programme was and remains a key issue for both small-holders and landless peasants. This is particularly so because of the lack of any formal social security system for the poor: they are wholly dependent on the land for their livelihood.

On the other hand, the MDC was established on the foundation of workers employed in the formal economy. The formal economy in Zimbabwe has traditionally employed about one million workers, originally one in four adults, but as the population has grown and formal employment shrunk, only one out of five adults is in formal employment today. Workers employed in the formal economy comprise a more privileged grouping than the peasantry, most of whom remain mired in deep poverty. However, it can be said the majority of supporters of both ZANU-PF and MDC are poor, and live below the poverty datum line.

The political conflicts that followed the formation of the MDC pitted the rural poor, mainly the peasantry, against the urban poor, mainly formal economy workers. MDC supporters were vilified by ZANU-PF as 'sell-outs' who supported a return to settler-colonialism and imperialism. The enthusiastic support of white farmers for the MDC made such an analysis easily credible.[3] The fact that workers who were employed in the formal economy were better off than peasants made such an accusation plausible, even though the worker's income and life-style were only marginally better than those of the peasant. The Fast Track Land Resettlement Programme was embarked upon soon after the formation of the MDC and proved to be a highly popular policy for the whole of the peasantry, in particular for the poor peasants who had little or no land. It was a highly astute political move, intended to enable ZANU-PF to regain the political support it had lost over the previous two decades, and it succeeded. It was all too easy to blame the poverty and unemployment poor people endured on the greed and racialism of whites, particularly of the white farmers, some of whom were regarded as harsh employers. Many white employers believed it was important to be 'tough' on workers, who would otherwise take advantage of any leniency. It was important to show who was 'boss'.

The land take-over led to the unilateral withdrawal of aid, known as 'sanctions' in ZANU-PF parlance and as 'targeted measures' by donors.[4] This meant that Zimbabwe was starved of foreign exchange beginning in 1998 up until 2010, affecting the economy negatively. Multilateral and bilateral donors were already hesitant about funding the Zimbabwe government as a result of its entry into the Democratic Republic of the Congo (DRC) war in 1998, the same year that discussions were being held between the government and donors through the UNDP on donor support for the resuscitation of the land resettlement programme. Zimbabwe had enjoyed an average of US\$250m of aid per annum since independence, and had become heavily donor dependent. Donor funds decreased markedly from 16.2% of the state budget in 1994–95 to zero by 2007 (see Table 1).

The utilisation of donor funds to influence policies and in this case also openly support 'regime change' is clear. There has been a tendency to blame all problems on the personality of Mugabe, so that change of leadership is seen as the key and essential change before donor funds are unblocked. It is not surprising that the personalities of different candidates received more prominence than their policies, knowledge, skills and experience.

The shortage of donor funds was one of the reasons for the policy of printing Zimbabwe dollars without matching the increased monetary supply either to foreign exchange holdings or to actual production, leading to the infamous hyper-inflation estimated at between 200 million and 500 billion per cent.[5] Hyper-inflation became more marked after 2003, when Dr Gideon Gono took over as Governor of the Reserve Bank. The value of the Zimbabwe dollar changed every day, and even within the same day. Coupled with the draconian arrests and imprisonment without trial of businessmen for charging 'exploitative' prices, producers soon gave up on production and retailers on selling. Shops became empty of produce. It was safer not to produce or sell anything than to produce food and other goods at a loss. Imprisonment without trial for shop-owners and managers was not an incentive to greater productivity. Producers and retailers took to selling their goods secretly, and

Table 1. Percentage of donor funds in state budget, 1994–2010

Year	%
1994–95	16.20
1995–96	10.20
1996–97	10.40
1997–98	7.50
1999	4.70
2000	3.43
2001	0.83
2002	0.80
2003	0.20
2004	0.40
2005	0.14
2006	0.05
2007	Nil
2008	Nil
2009	Nil
2010	36.0[a]

[a]The coalition government was promised US$810m, out of a total planned budget of US$2250m in 2010. This includes US$510m from the International Monetary Fund. However, by July 2010 only a tiny fraction of the promised assistance had been released to government, although a sizeable amount was available in terms of school textbooks and medicines.
Source: Minister of Finance, Budget Estimates, 1995–2010.

only in foreign exchange. The wealthy were still able to access basic foods, although it required some extra effort, such as driving to the next country or making special deals with producers or retailers. The poverty that had already been biting now became even more acute for the poor. Approximately half of the population became dependent on food aid after 2000.

It was in this situation of political polarisation, hyper-inflation and severe food shortages that the 2008 elections were held. Seeds, fertiliser and draught power were unavailable except to a few highly privileged politicians or soldiers. Most of the farmers who had recently been allocated land through the Fast Track Land Resettlement Programme could not use their land optimally as a result. This was compounded by six years of drought over the decade; 4.23 million hectares of land had gone to 127,000 small-holders by 2005, including teachers, civil servants, soldiers and policemen, while 24,000 large-scale farmers received 2.19 million hectares, with the dispossession of nearly 4000 white farmers.[6]

Elections as a Means towards Political Transformation

Given this background, ZANU-PF began to lose the hegemony that it had enjoyed between 1980 and 2000. In particular, its failure to support small-scale farmers, begun in the 1990s and continued after 2000, contradicted its land resettlement programme, yet small-scale farmers constituted the majority of the electorate. There was serious disillusionment in the power of voting to influence policies, direction and strategies. The participation of a larger percentage of voters in elections could radically change the voting patterns. Moreover, an estimated three million Zimbabweans have left the country, more than the total number of voters who have participated in elections since independence. If this diaspora were allowed to participate in elections, the results could be markedly different.

The formation of the MDC in 1999 saw an enthusiastic swing away from ZANU-PF. Although there were suspicions of electoral manipulation, the 2000 and March 2008 elections indicated that the MDC could poll as many votes or even more votes than ZANU-PF, although there was a dip in the 2005 elections (see Table 3).

From the numbers voting for ZANU-PF as compared with those voting for MDC, it is clear that the existence of two almost equally strong parties would result in a stalemate. The highly popular land resettlement programme that started in 2000 enabled ZANU-PF to recoup some of the support it had clearly lost in the 2000 referendum. The united and unequivocal front displayed by the war veterans and the armed forces in support of land resettlement since the 2000 elections ensured that ZANU-PF could retain substantial support, albeit severely curtailed when compared with its pre-1995 performance.

The Use of Violence to Influence Elections

Zimbabwean elections have always been characterised by violence, but the level of violence increased after 2000. It was particularly marked before the 27 June 2010 presidential re-run, when some 200 MDC activists were killed and some 40,000 people were displaced. Houses were burnt, crops and animals destroyed, and some 600 women raped. The violence was so extreme that Morgan Tsvangirai decided to withdraw from the re-run. By withdrawing he brought an end to the violence and killings, but he also conceded victory to Mugabe. There is a belief in some quarters that by utilising violence, the electorate will be forced to vote as directed. To some extent the 27 June 2010 presidential re-run appears to support this belief, with Mugabe winning 85.5% of the votes. The number of people who voted for him doubled from 1,079,730 to 2,150,269. However, only between 36.2 and 42.4%[7] of the

Table 2. Percentage of voters participating in elections[a]

	Total voters	Number who voted	% who voted
1990 House of Assembly	3,729,743	237,846	60.0
1995 House of Assembly	Unavailable	106,018	
2000 referendum	5,049,815[b]	1,312,338	26.0
2000 House of Assembly	5,049,815	2,493,925	49.4
2002 Presidential elections	5,654,184	3,046,891	53.89
2005 House of Assembly	5,658,624	2,696,670	47.7
2008 March 29 elections	5,934,768	2,537,240	42.75
2008 June 27 elections	5,934,768	2,514,750	42.4

[a]Note that the official number of registered voters is hotly disputed, with an estimate that approximately a quarter of those on the voters' roll are dead.
[b]Figure from 2000 Delimitation Report.
Source: Electoral Institute for the Sustainability of Democracy in Africa and Sokwanele (www.sokwanele.com).

Table 3. Percentage of votes for ZANU-PF and MDC

Year	Percentage vote for ZANU-PF	Percentage vote for MDC
1995 House of Assembly elections	81.4	Not yet formed
2000 Referendum[a]	45.3	54.7
2000 House of Assembly elections	48.6	47.0
2002 Presidential elections	56.0	42.1
2005 House of Assembly elections	59.6	39.5
March 2008 House of Assembly (MDC-T and MDC-M votes combined)[b]	45.8	53.8
March 2008 Presidential elections	43.2	47.9
June 2008 Presidential elections	85.5	Candidate withdrew

[a]The MDC organised against acceptance of the proposed constitution.
[b]Unfortunately the 2005 split of the MDC into two factions weakened their election victory.
Source: Electoral Institute for the Sustainability of Democracy in Africa and Sokwanele (www.sokwanele.com).

electorate participated, with a turnout of over 50% only in Mashonaland Central and Mashonaland East. It would appear that many voters chose to abstain.

The question is whether this violence will be repeated, and whether the population will be intimidated into voting according to the intimidators' instructions. The election violence in the 2000 elections was based almost entirely on the land resettlement question, with ZANU-PF asserting that it represented land for black people, whereas the MDC represented a return of all or some of the land to white commercial farmers. The Global Political Agreement of 2008–09 established a common policy on the land resettlement programme, viz. it cannot be reversed. This consensus means that the main reason for the use of violence has been removed. There are also indications that in many communities people are not prepared to vote for those who participated in violence against their community members. The utilisation of unemployed youths to perpetrate violence against their own communities has led to a drop in support for ZANU-PF, although this did not mean a commensurate increase in support for the MDC. Instead, it appears that a larger percentage of voters are abstaining from voting.

The Role of the Military in the Choice of Political Leadership

Since the early 1970s, when the armed struggle gained momentum, ZANU has experienced friction between the military and the political leadership. This conflict expressed itself particularly in the power struggle between Josiah Tongogara, head of Zimbabwe African National Liberation Army (ZANLA) in 1974–75 at the height of the Detente exercise, and Herbert Chitepo, Chairman of ZANU during that period. Chitepo was killed by a bomb in 1974. There is some evidence that he was killed by the Rhodesian Central Intelligence Organisation (CIO),[8] but this was contested within ZANU and ZANLA itself, where some groups contended that he was killed by factions from within ZANU. When Tongogara himself died in a car accident in 1979, just before independence, once again some elements within ZANU itself believed it was an assassination from within the ZANU leadership, which wanted to weaken the power of the military in the post-independence government, despite a very credible Mozambican government inquiry to the contrary. The 1970s' liberation struggle was primarily a military struggle, and at the time the military were the ultimate authority in the choice of leaders. Mugabe's election as president of ZANU was firmly supported by the military. After independence he continued to enjoy their support.

Several military leaders have refused to accept Tsvangirai as president, despite his electoral success. Tsvangirai again demonstrated his ability to win elections in the March 2008 presidential elections. The five-week delay in the announcement of the election results was interpreted as an attempt by military leaders to doctor the results so as to prevent Tsvangirai having an outright victory. The eventually announced results, through which Tsvangirai received 47.9% and Mugabe 43.2% of the votes, led to a re-run of the presidential election as a 50% plus one victory was needed for the presidential election to be decisive. MDC itself claimed that Tsvangirai had won 50.3% of the votes, but they were not able to assert their victory. Although it is difficult to prove foul play, the discrepancy in the number of voters recorded by non-governmental organisations as compared with the official Zimbabwe Electoral Commission (ZEC) figures of about 200,000 voters gives credence to this suspicion (source: http://www.sokwanele.com/election2008). A cursory analysis appears to show that the total number of voters was inflated, the additional votes going mainly to Tsvangirai and Makoni rather than to Mugabe, but by inflating the base it meant that Tsvangirai's tally was less than 50%. The army's alleged doctoring the elections, and the subsequent violence preceding the presidential re-run, underline once again the important role played by the armed forces in the choice of leaders. What the role of the armed forces will be in future elections will depend on how far their ideology and interests are represented by the various candidates and parties. Having played such an important role in the choosing of political leaders over the past 40 years, it is unlikely that their powers can be easily and speedily negated.

By 2008, given that Mugabe's continuation in power meant a continuation of the poor performance of the last decade, many people in both ZANU-PF and the MDC were looking for a way out of the dilemma posed by the military leaders' rejection of Tsvangirai. By 2008, nine years after the formation of the MDC, Tsvangirai had not been able to assuage the prejudice against him from the military leadership. There was a need for a presidential candidate who would be acceptable to the military. Simba Makoni's candidature provided exactly such a possibility.

The Role of 'War Veterans'

Freedom fighters played a critical role in the selection of their political leaders in the 1970s' guerrilla war. They remain a much feared group. ZANU-PF politicians have consistently tried to maintain control over this group since independence, and have managed it through the use of patronage and financing. Fear that war veterans could join hands with the opposition MDC was part of the reason for implementing the *Murambatsvina* clean-up in 2005, which seriously undermined the power of the urban poor. In the same year, the state initiated legislation that would deprive war veterans of their pensions if they involved themselves in politics, a stricture that is interpreted to mean joining the MDC. War veterans have triggered a number of crises, which culminated in policy changes. One such crisis was the 1997–98 war veterans' revolt against government leaders looting the War Veterans' Compensation Fund. This led to the sudden printing of money to pay war veterans compensation of Z$50,000 each, then about US$5,000. The Fast Track Land Resettlement of 2000 was initiated by war veterans, and was subsequently adopted as a policy by ZANU and the government as a whole. The controversial leadership of Joseph Chinotimba and Jabulani Sibanda of the War Veterans' Association is being challenged by a substantial number of war veterans, who contend that the two were teenagers during the 1970s liberation struggle and do not represent the welfare needs of genuine war veterans. The outcome of this struggle will affect the next elections. Chinotimba and Sibanda are implicated in the violence that preceded the presidential re-run, perpetrated by youths led by military and paramilitary leaders.

The Role of the Business Community

The business community plays a significant role in politics through its financial ability to support different parties and players. Generally the business community has played 'safe' by supporting all parties. It supported ZANU-PF enthusiastically, but the post-2000 developments within ZANU-PF allowed the poor to take over not only white-owned commercial farms, but also a significant number of black-owned farms. Some of the urban poor, supported by certain ZANU-PF leaders, were also threatening to take over urban businesses. The ZANU-PF government blamed the business community for the hyper-inflation, imposing price controls and imprisoning business owners and managers without trial for price increases. This anti-business stance meant that the business community was looking for an alternative political leadership that could adequately support their interests. They were more likely to support a fellow businessman such as Simba Makoni than a trade unionist such as Morgan Tsvangirai.

The Role of the Rural Population

As the rural population comprises 68% of the population, its vote can be critical. Up until 2000 the rural voters overwhelmingly supported ZANU-PF, but the 2000 elections brought about a rude awakening. Whoever wins the next presidential elections will need rural support.

Potential Presidential Candidates

It was not surprising that the 2008 elections had the potential to bring about a sea change in Zimbabwean politics. The loss of direction by ZANU-PF from the early 1990s had led to a weakening of its hegemony. There was little prospect of a change of leadership within ZANU-PF. For over a decade there had been various internal attempts within ZANU-PF to effect a succession plan through the Politburo, the Central Committee, and a Party Congress, and all of these had failed. Instead leadership rivalry had exacerbated disunity within the party, with ethnic loyalties, business rivalries and patronage leading to a dangerous and debilitating stalemate.

One faction within ZANU-PF was led by General Solomon Mujuru, the first head of the army after independence, and one of the most outstanding guerrilla leaders in the 1960s–1970s war. Another faction was led by Emmerson Mnangagwa, one of the first guerrillas to operate within Rhodesia. His participation in the liberation struggle began in the early 1960s when he was a teenager. It is difficult to define clear-cut ideological differences between these two factions, but there are ethnic and personality differences.

Mujuru played a key role in ensuring that the freedom fighters of the military wing of ZANU, the ZANLA, of which he was *de facto* leader between 1975 and 1976, accepted the political leadership of Robert Mugabe. Mugabe thus owes his acceptance by the military to Mujuru, who incidentally belongs to the same ethnic sub-group, the Zezuru, within the larger Shona ethnic group. At the time, the choice was between Ndbaningi Sithole, elected President of ZANU in 1963, a Manyika, another Shona sub-group, and Robert Mugabe, who was the next most senior member in the ZANU leadership.

After independence, Mujuru headed the Zimbabwe National Army up until 1992, when he resigned to devote himself to his private businesses. He is a capitalist mogul, with extensive agricultural, mining and other business enterprises, including an internet trading and money transfer business. He is known as a brilliant political strategist. He has himself denied having any presidential ambitions, yet he is believed to be a 'king maker'. On the other hand, while he has supported his wife Joice's candidature as Vice-President, with presumably the potential for her to become the next President, there is some unease at having such a powerful husband in the background.

Joice Mujuru joined the 1970s liberation struggle as a schoolgirl, and rose within the ranks of ZANLA to become a military commander. After independence, she became one of the youngest ministers in the Cabinet, and has served in government for the past 30 years in various capacities. She has also improved her academic qualifications consistently from O levels, to A levels, a university diploma, a Bachelor's degree and a Master's degree. She is currently enrolled on a PhD course. She is known as a hard-working, conscientious and wise decision-maker, who is known to take up the advice of the experts in her ministries. She is an astute politician.

Mujuru is also believed to have favoured Simba Makoni as a compromise candidate within ZANU-PF for the position of president for many years, but this was never accepted by Mugabe or by the decision-making bodies within ZANU-PF. Mujuru is an outspoken critic of some of Mugabe's decisions, including entry of Zimbabwe into the DRC war and the use of violence against ZANU-PF supporters in Mashonaland areas won by ZANU-PF parliamentarians and senators in 2008.

Mnangagwa has been seen as Mugabe's favourite succession candidate. Mnangagwa belongs to the Karanga ethnic group, one of the most powerful Shona ethnic sub-groups. Mnangagwa was recruited as a ZAPU guerrilla in 1962 from Zambia, and was sentenced to death for criticising Joshua Nkomo at the military training camp in Iringa, Tanzania, by a tribunal chaired by Dumiso Dabengwa. His life was saved by the intervention of Leopold Takawira and Simon Muzenda, both Karangas, and both of whom broke away from ZAPU to form ZANU in 1963. From Iringa, Mnangagwa went on to train in Egypt and China, to return to the country in 1964. On his return he was a key member of the Crocodile Group, the first guerrilla incursion that led to the death of a white farmer, Oberholzer. He was in charge of blowing up a train in Masvingo, then known as Fort Victoria. Mnangagwa was arrested, and escaped the mandatory death penalty because he was deemed to be under-age.[9] Instead, he was sentenced to 10 years' imprisonment, mainly at Khami Maximum Security Prison. On being released from prison he went on to study for a law degree at the University of Zambia. He returned to the liberation struggle in 1976 as a ZANU headquarters advisor to Robert Mugabe in Maputo in Mozambique.

Mnangagwa is believed to have been instrumental in persuading Mugabe to enter the DRC war in 1998, and was named by the United Nations as the main beneficiary of the diamond export from the DRC under cover of the war. However, his prospects became clouded as a result of the alleged Tsholotsho political 'coup' spearheaded by his ally, Jonathan Moyo, to position Mnangagwa as Mugabe's successor. This plan failed, with the removal of key Mnangagwa supporters from the ZANU-PF leadership. Mnangagwa is also regarded as 'unelectable' as a result of losing two parliamentary elections to a little known MDC candidate, Blessing Chebundo, in 2000 and 2005. The Tsholotsho debacle led to the promotion of Mujuru's wife, Joice, to the position of Vice-President of the country. Mnangagwa was appointed as the Minister of Defence under the Unity Government in February 2009, giving him a key position in terms of control over the armed forces.

Mnangagwa's rise to prominence again after 2007 is perceived to be partially a result of his rival, General Mujuru, continuously trying to organise a peaceful succession plan within ZANU-PF. The latest such attempt was at the special congress in 2007. Mujuru's strategy failed. Mujuru's position weakened further as Mugabe publicly attacked his Vice-President, Joice Mujuru, apparently for utilising her position to benefit her husband's private business interests.

The inability of ZANU-PF to resolve the succession struggle opened the way for new developments. The main candidate to inherit the mantle of the presidency was Morgan Tsvangirai, President of the Movement for Democratic Change, formed in 1999. Tsvangirai became prominent because of his immense courage in the face of violent persecution, torture and political assassinations of opposition members. Such courage was certainly essential for anyone willing to oppose the hegemony of ZANU-PF, as the general perception is that any critic from within or from outside the party will be killed.

In terms of ideology and policies Tsvangirai is known for his flexibility and pragmatism, as shown by his ability to establish the MDC on the basis of trade union support, and soon after his ability to shape MDC policies on the basis of white commercial farmer requirements, as enunciated by his chief economic advisor and planner, Eddie Cross. In 2004, he was trapped into an alleged attempt to assassinate Mugabe, leading to an expensive show trial. He was defended by George Bizos, a South African human rights lawyer who was part of the team that defended South African freedom leaders in the famous South African Rivonia Trial. Tsvangirai was found not guilty. The show trial displayed the ZANU-PF government's desire for political legitimacy, nationally and internationally, by utilising the justice system to discredit its rival. The prolonged trial period meant that the MDC's political mobilisation for the 2005 elections was severely hampered, as it had to spend money, time and effort on the trial. At the same time, Tsvangirai was periodically on the run and imprisoned during the period. Despite severe persecution, he continued to lead the opposition. The show trial had its intended impact: while the MDC had won 47% of the votes in the 2000 parliamentary elections, it won only 39.52% of the votes in the 2005 parliamentary elections. ZANU-PF, on the other hand, was gradually losing the large majority that it had enjoyed in the first two decades after independence.

Despite Tsvangirai and the MDC's popularity among urban workers, its strategies for improvement of workers' living conditions were confined to strikes, which were brutally suppressed by the armed forces. Workers found that going on strike did not bring in any improvements in their dire living conditions and high level of unemployment, but could lead to draconian outcomes, and possibly death. The other strategy of gaining power through elections also eluded the MDC, as their election results failed to be decisive. The result was a stalemate. There was room for a third leadership alternative, and this came in the person of Simba Makoni and a new political movement, the Mavambo Kusile Dawn Movement.

Many individuals as well as groups were dissatisfied with the political landscape of two large opposing forces, with very similar structures and policies, fighting for political dominance, often through violent fights led by gangs of unemployed youths, who were paid handsomely to beat up and at times even rape and kill members of the opposition. The political polarisation was extreme, with rampant and open warfare being waged by the ZANU-PF militia against its opponents, while the MDC believed the right reaction was to fight violence with violence. Armed aggression and armed resistance were the strategies of the day.

Moreover, there were party members from both ZANU-PF and the MDC who were dissatisfied with the parties they were in, but were not prepared to join the opposing party. Some ZANU-PF members were disappointed because they had not been able to obtain high positions through elections, as a popularly elected candidate could be replaced by someone chosen by the top leadership. This had become rampant within ZANU-PF, and the practice had also begun to seep into the MDC. A substantial number were dissatisfied with the fact that Robert Mugabe had remained in power for several decades, with visible signs of loss of policy direction and innovativeness. Mugabe remained the compromise candidate in the succession battles being waged within ZANU-PF. There were several ZANU-PF leaders who were not prepared to challenge Mugabe openly, but nevertheless saw the need for change. They could support Simba Makoni and the movement he had established, Mavambo Kusile Dawn,[10] without necessarily being called a 'sell-out'.

In 2005, the MDC split into two factions, one led by Morgan Tsvangirai and the other by Arthur Mutambara. The MDC split can be analysed as partially a split between the workers who remained loyal to Tsvangirai, and the intellectuals, who followed Welshman Ncube and Arthur Mutambara. As the majority in the party were workers, Tsvangirai remained with the larger portion of the original party, but deprived to some extent of its intellectual and professional foundations based on university student and lecturer support. Some MDC members felt dissatisfied with the dominance of the workers on the one hand, and of the white farmers on the other hand, within the party. They were also dissatisfied with having Tsvangirai, a trade unionist and a worker, as the top leader, rather than someone who was either a rich business tycoon or a renowned intellectual. They believed that Tsvangirai did not offer the right leadership in terms of money and intellect. Instead it was believed that his financial supporters, particularly the white commercial farmers, were powerful decision-makers in the party. The dominance of the white commercial farmers within the organisation proved to be divisive.

The Entry of New Political Players: The Mavambo Kusile Dawn Movement

It was not surprising that the dissatisfied individuals from both ZANU-PF and MDC-T[11] were soon to come together to support Simba Makoni, a former finance minister under ZANU-PF who was dismissed in 2002 by Robert Mugabe for supporting the devaluation of the Zimbabwe currency, as a surprise candidate for the presidency, in opposition to Robert Mugabe and Morgan Tsvangirai. As soon as Makoni announced his candidature on 5 February 2008, seven weeks before the election date, a substantial number of volunteers appeared, including many defectors from the two major parties. Numerous agents from the CIO[12] also rushed forward to offer themselves as 'volunteers'.

Much interest was based on the personality of Simba Makoni. He has a reputation of being courageous, in that he had openly critiqued policies and statements enunciated by Mugabe during his first and second periods in Cabinet. Promoted as Deputy Minister of Agriculture at the age of 30 at independence, he was promoted to Minister of Industry and Energy Development between 1981 and 1983, when he left government to become the Executive Secretary of the Southern African Development Community (SADC). He held this position up until 1994. He was again appointed as a Cabinet Minister in 2000 as Minister of Finance, but was removed in 2002.

His main reputation is that of a technocrat, with a sophisticated understanding of development, foreign relations and economics. He is not reputed to be a politician, a great advantage to him in a situation where most Zimbabweans have developed a serious distrust of politicians, who are suspected of being ruthless, corrupt and willing as well as able to kill their opponents. Moreover, a large proportion of Zimbabweans respect leaders with a high level of education and a reputation as a technocrat. Of the potential leaders on offer, Makoni is one of the most educated, holding a PhD in Chemistry from Leicester University. He also has the advantage of having been a ZANU student leader, ZANU representative and fund-raiser in Europe in the 1970s. Despite coming from within ZANU-PF, he has had the courage to stand up against ZANU-PF's policies and actions, and to leave the party to form an opposition movement. His ZANU-PF past enabled him to garner some of the support that ZANU-PF traditionally enjoyed. Moreover, Makoni was in a position to bring in a larger percentage of the electorate to the polls. A further advantage was that he could be in a position to have the support of the military. He was rumoured to have the support of General Mujuru and other top military leaders. Rumours flowed round the country that Mujuru was firmly behind Simba Makoni, and would come out into the open in due course. As it turned out, Mujuru did not come out into the open. However, there was no doubt that he had previously provided such support, and was still regarded as a secret supporter.

There was also a flood of finance. Some of this came from individual and distraught Zimbabwean citizens in the diaspora who wanted a change from the polarised and violent political scene. Business interests in Zimbabwe contributed generously, as the ZANU-PF regime had been so hostile to business, particularly to the banking sector. International business interests who wanted to enter or maintain their business interests in Zimbabwe contributed. The two main centres for the collection of funds were South Africa and the United Kingdom, both of which had large numbers of Zimbabweans.[13]

A significant proportion of ZANU-PF supporters were prepared to vote for Makoni in preference to Mugabe. He was seen as a younger, technically competent representative of ZANU-PF. The supposed support from the military strengthened this impression. Moreover, some members of ZANU-PF within the ZANU-PF strongholds of Mashonaland had agreed on a strategy known as 'kick the ball out of the football field'. This strategy, based on football imagery, meant they were urging voters to vote for ZANU-PF for all positions except that of the presidency; and indeed this occurred, with many ZANU-PF strongholds voting for ZANU-PF councillors, members of parliament and senators, but not for Mugabe as president. While it was a successful strategy for achieving the aim of winning seats for ZANU-PF but ensuring that Mugabe could not get sufficient votes to be elected as president, it had a deadly post-election outcome for the communities within these areas, as they became victims of intimidation, torture, rapes and killings after they had successfully voted against Mugabe. Having voted for ZANU-PF, they found themselves being targeted as enemies by youths led by some war veterans and some members of the armed forces.

The fact that Makoni came from within ZANU-PF was a matter of concern for MDC supporters, who saw him as a ZANU-PF plant to deflect support from Tsvangirai. Rumours abounded that President Mugabe had himself asked Makoni to stand as a way of 'stealing' votes away from Tsvangirai. In such a situation, the dedicated MDC supporters were overtly opposed to Makoni and remained firmly behind Tsvangirai. The smaller MDC faction under Mutambara, however, immediately chose to support Makoni's bid.

The March 2008 harmonised elections were peaceful, and were marked by the renewed enthusiasm of voters, who saw the entry of a potentially strong opposition from within ZANU-PF as a serious challenge to the ZANU-PF itself. This might bring about the end of the impasse between the MDC and ZANU-PF. This view was strengthened by the virulent attacks made by Mugabe himself against Makoni, whom he called a 'prostitute' and a ' noisy frog', that is, making much noise but not able to pose a real threat.

Makoni faced several problems. These included the dependence on 'volunteers' instead of a strong party structure that characterised both the MDC and ZANU-PF. Many of these 'volunteers' were highly independent individualists. There were also plants from both of the big parties, as well as from the CIO, Zimbabwe's powerful secret service. Many volunteers had their own private agendas. They supported Makoni without sharing a political vision. The fact that he had only seven weeks to organise for the elections displayed Makoni's risk-taking personality: although he was unlikely to win, he was in a position to break the political jam. Dumiso Dabengwa rightly summarised the situation thus: neither Mugabe nor Tsvangirai could win an outright majority if there was a credible third candidate. He has asserted that this was his reason for supporting Makoni.[14] In this situation, it is clear that if the 207,470 votes for Makoni were added to the tallies of either Mugabe or Tsvangirai, it would be sufficient to bring about indisputable victory.

Prior to the March and June 2008 elections, Makoni made strenuous efforts to meet with Tsvangirai in order to organise a joint strategy, but he was continuously rebuffed. Makoni was in the position of being able to throw in his support for Tsvangirai and the MDC for the re-run, which he was urged to do by some of his followers, but he was unwilling to do this without some dialogue with Tsvangirai.

After the two elections, Makoni faced internal opposition led by Ibbo Mandaza and Major Kudzai Mbudzi, two of his major supporters. This leadership challenge was based on the utilisation of Mavambo Kusile Dawn (MKD) resources. His opponents wanted to take control of the resources that had been contributed to the movement, but Makoni was not willing to allow them to do so. Part of the problem was the secrecy necessitated by the political situation in Zimbabwe, with donors unwilling to expose themselves openly. Another problem was the nature of MKD itself, consisting of volunteers who did not have a common ideological foundation or direction. Moreover, the speed at which MKD was formed meant that there had not been sufficient time to build a foundation based on trust and in-depth knowledge of members.

Makoni was able to transform MKD from a movement into a political party in July 2009. Since then it has been organising as a party at grassroots level. The vision of MKD is a stable, peaceful, united, progressive and developed Zimbabwe, where the rights and freedoms of all citizens are respected and protected. Its mission statement is to mobilise the nation to share and realise the vision of constant renewal, inclusion, tolerance, transparency and accountability. Its philosophy is to create an open, accessible, accountable, responsible and responsive governance system that provides genuine empowerment, which is caring and compassionate, and which provides equity and fairness for all Zimbabweans, regardless of region, ethnicity, religion, gender, race, class, disability and age. Its principles include:

- A democratic non-racial party and country, promoting gender equality and the welfare of all citizens.
- The supremacy of and respect for the Constitution and laws of Zimbabwe.
- The separation of legislative, executive and judicial powers, while engendering effective cooperation between them.
- Clear division between the office bearers, functions, institutions and resources of political parties and those of the State.
- Representative, responsive and accountable government chosen through regular, peaceful, free and fair elections.
- Guaranteeing the right of all citizens of Zimbabwe resident outside the country to participate in elections.
- Decentralisation of government authority and responsibility as close as possible to the people it is expected to serve.
- Respect for all legitimate rights, including religious and cultural rights, of individuals, associations and communities within a secular state.
- The right of all people to property and assets in a regulated market economy with protection for vulnerable groups.

- Improvement in the quality of life of all Zimbabweans through increased access to housing, health, education and the protection of all people from crime and violence.
- Protection and enhancement of the quality of the physical environment and natural resource base.[15]

These carefully thought-out principles definitely have appeal for young, educated voters, but have as yet to prove attractive to the less educated populace. In particular, the large rural population is more interested in concrete bread and butter issues than in more abstract principles.

Conclusion

Makoni has the potential to come into power, benefiting in particular from the institutional decay within ZANU-PF. ZANU-PF began to weaken in the early 1990s. One reason was the Unity Agreement of 1987 between ZANU-PF and ZAPU, which turned the country into a one-party state, with little criticism of anything done by the government. There was no longer any real opposition. The adoption of the Economic Structural Adjustment (ESAP) contributed to the decay. ESAP was supposed to bring about a spurt of economic growth by doing away with uncompetitive local industries, and instead concentrating on Zimbabwe's competitive advantages. In the event, there was a long period of de-industrialisation, which is still continuing, and concentration of the economy only on mining, the one area in which Zimbabwe and many other African countries have a comparative advantage. With de-industrialisation came a drastic lowering of formal sector employment. The violent take-over of land after 2000 contributed to the loss of commercially viable crops for export such as tobacco and horticulture, as well as loss of wheat and dairy production. It also led indirectly to a drastic shortage of maize, the staple food, through the government's decision to place most funding on large-scale rather than on small-scale farming, while removing subsidies for basic agricultural inputs. This led to a dire shortage of maize seeds and fertiliser. The influx of food aid from countries with highly subsidised agriculture further weakened the small farmers, as such food imports could be half or even a third of production costs in Zimbabwe itself. Thus, the economic downturn led directly to the conviction that political change was essential and unavoidable.

Makoni is regarded as a ZANU-PF protégé, but unscarred by the corruption and cynicism that has come to characterise that institution. Thus, his election would be seen as a continuation of the better aspects of ZANU-PF. If he is able to maintain this squeaky-clean image, his chances for election as an individual will be good. The success of his party will depend on the effectiveness of its grassroots organisation.

Moreover, his potential support from the military and from the business community will be of critical importance. Another factor is the three million-strong diaspora. They are not able to vote at present. Should they overcome this difficulty, the electoral patterns are likely to change. The diaspora may find MKD an attractive alternative to both ZANU-PF and the MDC.

So far Makoni has not managed to win over the large rural community, although this large grouping has become sceptical of ZANU-PF's ability to pull the country out of its economic morass. This scepticism has grown after the violence meted out to its own supporters in the three Mashonaland provinces after their refusal to vote overwhelmingly for Mugabe. Even traditional leaders, who usually support ZANU-PF and the government unquestioningly, have been critical of the violence meted out to their subjects, and many have taken steps to prevent further repetition of such transgressions.

Makoni will also benefit from the confused situation within the MDC itself, in terms of policies, direction and leadership challenges. The coalition government period has witnessed growing public disenchantment with the MDC, as it has been unable to wrest control of key areas from ZANU-PF control. Internal corruption and bickering have added to the disenchantment.

Large numbers of Zimbabweans are desperately searching for a solution to Zimbabwe's problems. The emergence of a third credible party offers some respite from the endemic political polarisation. Although a speedy solution to the Zimbabwean impasse is unlikely, the move away from polarisation is a step forward. Moreover, the need for practical solutions to real problems, such as the need for clean water and adequate sewage systems, has led to the establishment of some consensus from all parties. The development of such consensus has been helped by the end of the polarisation, which has been helped by the formation of the unity government and by the entry of MKD into the dialogue.

Notes

1. ZANU later changed its name to Zimbabwe African National Union Patriotic Front (ZANU-PF), after a short-lived pre-independence coalition, known as the Patriotic Front, with ZAPU. ZAPU has retained its original name.
2. Net primary school enrolments fell from 98.5% in 2002 to 97% in 2003 to 91% in 2009 (CSO, 2006; CSO and UNICEF, 2009; Poverty Assessment Study Survey (PASS II)). The percentage of women who could not access professional assistance at childbirth rose from 23% in 1999 to 31% in 2005/06 up to 39% in 2009. This resulted in an increase of maternal mortality from less than 300 in 1994 to 725 in 2009 per 100,000 women (CSO, 2007; CSO and UNICEF, 2009).
3. White commercial farmers were enthusiastic supporters of ZANU-PF in the 1980s, when it became evident that the ZANU-PF government was not going to take over their farms. However, by the late 1990s ZANU-PF was facing increasing criticism from war veterans who accused the government of betraying the objectives of the liberation struggle, the chief of which was land redistribution. ZANU-PF leaders were themselves being accused of being 'sell-outs' who had feathered their own nests, and forgotten the war veterans' demands for land and employment. The ZANU-PF leadership were quick to respond to the war veterans' demands, in order to regain their political dominance, and tried to negotiate with white farmers to give up a substantial proportion of their land-holdings. White farmers were largely reluctant to give up their lands. Nor were donors prepared to fund the exercise in a timely fashion, mainly because the demand for a resuscitation of the land resettlement programme coincided with the entry of Zimbabwe into the DRC war in 1998. Western donors generally did not support Zimbabwe's entry into the DRC war, and used their financial muscle to affect Zimbabwe government policies. Political exigencies led to the establishment of the Fast Tract Land Resettlement Programme through which about 90% of the 13 million hectares of land held by about 4500 white farmers was unilaterally taken over by government for redistribution. Figures from Mahmood Mamdani (2008, p. 8, http://www.lrb.co.uk/v30/n23/mahmood-mamdani/lessons-of-zimbabwe).
4. Donors utilise the term 'sanctions' for travel restrictions to European Union countries and the United States against some 200 ZANU-PF political leaders.
5. Two hundred million per cent is the conservative estimate of the Zimbabwe government (CSO, which is now known as ZIMSTATS, 2009), whereas 500 billion per cent is the estimate of the International Monetary Fund (2010).

6. The larger percentage of land went to civil servants and the armed forces, as has been shown through the research done by Ian Scoones (2008). Scoones's research in Masvingo shows that 14% of the land went to civil servants, mainly teachers and extension workers, 5% to business people, and 3% to security forces. Sixty per cent were defined as 'ordinary farmers' from nearby Communal Areas.
7. Percentage figures differ according to different sources.
8. Ken Flower, head of the CIO during this period, makes the claim that the CIO managed to kill Chitepo, and also managed to utilise internal conflicts within ZANU to lay the blame on ZANU itself. See Flower (1987, pp. 147–150).
9. Information from Ngwabi Bhebe (2004, pp. 137–140).
10. *Mavambo* is Shona and *Kusile* is Ndebele for 'dawn' or 'new beginning'.
11. MDC-T is the name of the faction under Morgan Tsvangirai.
12. The CIO is the Zimbabwe Secret Service, and operates directly under the President's Office. One of its tasks is to infiltrate all political parties, particularly opposition parties. As the Mavambo.Kusile Dawn movement welcomed all volunteers, it was inevitable that it would be heavily infiltrated by CIO agents.
13. There are an estimated three million Zimbabweans in South Africa and about half a million in the United Kingdom.
14. Dumiso Dabengwa in a speech to ZAPU, on 1 July 2010, www.zimeye.org
15. Summarised from the Mavambo Kusile Dawn (2009) Principles and Policies flyer, Harare.

References

Bhebe, N. (2004) *Simon Vengayi Muzenda and the Struggle for and Liberation of Zimbabwe* (Gweru: Mambo Press).

Central Statistics Office (2006) *2003 Poverty Assessment Study Survey (PASS II)* (Harare: Central Statistics Office).

Central Statistics Office (2007) *Zimbabwe Demographic and Health Survey 2005–2006* (Harare: Central Statistics Office).

Central Statistics Office and UNICEF (2009) *Multiple Indicator Monitoring Survey* (Harare: Central Statistics Office and UNICEF).

Flower, K. (1987) *Serving Secretly* (London: John Murray).

Mamdani, M. (2008) Lessons of Zimbabwe, *London Review of Books*, 20(23), pp. 17–21.

Minister of Finance (1995–2010) Budget Estimates, 1995–2010, Parliament of Zimbabwe, Harare.

Scoones, I. (2008) A new start for Zimbabwe, http:www.lair.org.za/news/a-new-start-for-zimbabwe-by-ian-schoones.html/

The Consequences of Violent Politics in Norton, Zimbabwe

JOCELYN ALEXANDER* AND KUDAKWASHE CHITOFIRI**
*University of Oxford, Oxford, UK
**University of Zimbabwe, Harare, Zimbabwe

ABSTRACT   *The lasting consequences of violent politics in Zimbabwe cannot be fully grasped without exploring both their institutional and material contexts and local interpretations of the meaning of particular acts of violence. Drawing on narratives of political violence from the town of Norton, three points are made. First, the extreme electoral violence of 2008 was interpreted by opposition members as an almost inexplicable moment of rupture. As a result, it damaged social relations in lasting ways. Second, the powerful link between the ruling party's coercive politics and people's livelihoods in a context of economic collapse meant that violence had deeply damaging effects on every aspect of people's lives from which many have not yet recovered. Third, regardless of their party affiliation, people's political relations with Zimbabwe's Inclusive Government, established in 2009, have been powerfully shaped by their understandings of the material and other obligations constituted through violence and suffering in previous years.*

Introduction

Studies of political violence in post-2000 Zimbabwe have painted a detailed picture of human rights abuses perpetrated overwhelmingly by the ZANU-PF government and its allies, including war veterans and youth militia.[1] This violence is—convincingly—portrayed as centrally orchestrated, focused on political opponents, and ideologically framed.[2] It is thus not the ethnic, decentralised and patronage-driven violence stereotypically associated with much of Africa, and it has as a result a different geography of blame and accountability, focused centrally on the state and ruling party. The concern in much of the Zimbabwean literature to document perpetrators and victims in a human rights framework—to establish what Shari Eppel (2009) calls a 'forensic truth'—is essential in a host of contexts, not least the judicial context. However, it also obscures a great deal of complexity in the meanings assigned to violence, and therefore its salience in people's ongoing relations and politics. Eppel (2009, p. 969) calls for attention to the 'local narratives and moral debates over the allocation of blame, and the intricate web of actors and artefacts these can incorporate'. Such stories are shaped by local histories, beliefs and social and material relations that together work to mediate the consequences of violence.

Drawing on a study of the town of Norton, we argue that local social norms, practices of political mobilisation, and an increasingly politicised and ruinous economy powerfully shaped the nature and consequences of political violence in the last few years. We focus on three points: the first is the rupture in social norms occasioned by the extreme electoral violence of 2008 which, though not one-sided, weighed overwhelmingly on the opposition Movement for Democratic Change (MDC). In contrast to previous episodes, this violence rendered kin and neighbours 'unknowable', and shaped their subsequent interactions. Our second point is that political violence, though centrally directed and ideologically framed, was also importantly shaped by socio-economic and institutional networks and relations of patronage. These had taken on profound importance for people's well-being in the context of the escalating economic collapse that devastated Zimbabwe after 2000. Economic collapse created vulnerabilities as well as bonds and obligations that were important in moulding opposition politics and determining the costs of activism. For the ruling party, patronage relations were built on the back of state resources and shaped both loyalty and the organisation of violence. Our third point is that, for activists in both parties, these material relations played a central role in reshaping political discourse and expectations after the signing of the Global Political Agreement in September 2008 paved the way for the formation of an 'Inclusive Government'—in which the MDC and ZANU-PF sat side by side—in early 2009 (see Cheeseman and Tendi, 2010).

In exploring these issues we draw on interviews carried out in 2009 and 2010, largely with MDC activists in Norton but also with a small number of ZANU-PF supporters. Names used below have been changed save where figures hold prominent public office, such as parliamentary seats.

Violence and Social Norms in 2008

Political violence was not new to Norton in 2008. The town is home to some 45,000 people and located 40 kilometres west of the capital Harare. As in other urban areas, it has had a strong MDC presence from the time of the party's formation in 1999 owing to the existence of trade union, cooperative and civic organisations as well as its close ties to the capital where the MDC was at its most powerful. ZANU-PF had mounted violent challenges to the MDC, notably during elections, since 2000, but had been unable to dislodge it. Here as elsewhere, however, the violence that marked the interim between the 'harmonised' parliamentary and presidential elections of 29 March 2008, in which the MDC emerged victorious, and the presidential run-off on 27 June 2008 was unprecedented in the post-2000 period.

MDC supporters in Norton had greeted the announcement of the March 2008 results with euphoria. Many well-known ZANU-PF supporters had initially publicly congratulated their MDC rivals.[3] It was only a few weeks later, however, that ZANU-PF began systematically to organise a new onslaught of violence. The sudden turn of events underlined its centrally organised nature. In keeping with many other areas, a military figure was at the heart of the process. A retired senior member of the army known simply as 'the colonel' to MDC supporters moved into Norton's Katanga township in early June and assumed leadership of the ZANU-PF hierarchy. His white Mitsubishi truck rapidly became a source of terror: MDC activists spoke of being overwhelmed by feelings of panic whenever they saw such a truck long after the worst of the violence had ended.[4] The colonel organised 'bases' in each of Norton's 15 wards. ZANU-PF youth[5] and committee leaders ran the bases, assuming military titles such as Brigadier and Captain, and received support from war veterans and security forces. In June, lists of MDC activists were compiled and ZANU-PF youth set about rounding up, interrogating, beating and torturing MDC activists in (and outside) the bases. ZANU-PF women cooked in the bases and brought firewood to them, as well as being called upon in some instances to punish women MDC activists.

ZANU-PF considered a failure to participate in the activities at the bases as 'criminal' and deserving of punishment. Many parents sent their children to the bases as protection against attacks on their persons and property. Well-known MDC supporters were 'encouraged' to attend the bases. Once there, they were made to condemn the MDC, to renounce any further involvement with it, and to burn their party cards and regalia in front of large audiences. Voluntarily attending the bases was no protection against violence. One young man, who had been an active ZANU-PF youth in Norton before joining the MDC while away working in Bulawayo, returned during the election period and voluntarily denounced the MDC at a base. He had been promised by ZANU-PF youths that he would not be harmed if he did so. He was none the less beaten so severely that he required hospitalisation for over a week.[6]

Many people simply fled Norton in the face of these attacks or went into hiding. MDC youth did not, however, accept this treatment without objection. In mid-June, they launched a violent attack on three bases, stoning, beating and chasing away the ZANU-PF occupants before they found themselves outnumbered and forced into retreat. Over 50 MDC supporters were subsequently arrested by police, a response that had been notably absent in regard to previous ZANU-PF violence.[7] Further retaliation by ZANU-PF followed.

Norton is a small town in which people are well known to one another. Despite their divided political loyalties, social relations—born of kinship, workplaces, neighbourhoods, and other associations—had worked to constrain if not eliminate violence among town residents, and to mitigate that carried out by outsiders and state agents. The shocking aspect of the violence of June 2008 for many MDC members lay in the grotesque betrayal of the norms that governed Norton's social relations. This violation of what was considered normal behaviour had the effect of rendering violence inexplicable. Nathan, an MDC activist in his mid-20s, explained his experience. He had pulled over in his brother's car at a Norton shopping centre in order to help a friend with car trouble when several ZANU-PF youths approached and told him that two ZANU-PF base commanders, Marcus and Brian, wanted to see him. After some time, he drove to the beer-hall where the two were waiting for him. Despite knowing that they were directly involved in organising violence and running bases, Nathan went without fear:

> You see we grew up together with these guys. I even considered them my big brothers because they grew up playing with my brother.[8] I never thought they would do anything to hurt me. I actually thought they wanted to warn me of danger ... [W]hen I arrived at where these guys were, I saw that it was quite a big group of Zanu youths and they were drinking beer. Marcus started questioning me about my brother [a senior MDC activist] and his involvement with the MDC and that they had heard that the car he was driving once belonged to [MDC MP] Nelson Chamisa. They actually said that we were related to Chamisa and that my brother ... was responsible for spreading the MDC gospel in Norton and for selling the MDC album [a CD of pro-MDC songs]. I tried to reason with him but he then said that my case can only be finished at the base because my name was on the hit list and could only be removed if I went with him and he would apologise on my behalf to his superiors for my behaviour ... He even promised that as long as I went with him to the base nothing would happen to me. At the base I was asked all sorts of questions and accused of distributing MDC campaign material and for celebrating when Musumbu [the MDC MP for Norton] won the 29 March parliamentary elections. I was at the base from around 7:30 pm to 3 am and was severely assaulted with sticks, sjambocks, and iron bars. I was even made to carry a hot pot of sadza on my head and was forced to lie down on my stomach whilst they were beating my feet. Around past 3 am I was then carried by [the white Mitsubishi] truck to the police station where the colonel, who was driving the car, told the police that I should be arrested for mutilating campaign posters and for writing obscenities about Mugabe on the wall.[9]

Nathan believed that Marcus had paid a high price for his violent abrogation of social norms: 'I strongly suspect that he is no longer stable. If you watch him now he looks like a person who is being haunted by something and to be honest with you I don't feel pity for him at all. Every time you go to the shops he is there looking for money to buy scuds [opaque beer]. He surely has no shame—sometime in April he came home begging [my brother] to assist him with transport to ferry his sister's body to the mortuary and we provided him with the vehicle because I know that he is capable of thinking, he is having a hard time in his own mind.'[10]

Nathan had considered going to a ritual specialist in order to have Marcus bewitched, but felt bound not to do so by his beliefs and longstanding relationship with Marcus: 'It's just that I'm a Christian and we grew up [together].' In the months after the violence, both Nathan and Marcus struggled to find an explanation for what had happened. Nathan had asked Marcus directly to account for his behaviour in the base: 'He tried as much as he could to explain why he did what he did and he said it was because we were in a war and that he could not explain what had possessed him to do what he did. And honestly I think there must have been a bad spirit thrown into the country by Bob [Mugabe] that caused people to behave like animals. You see, people had their brothers and sisters severely beaten at the bases.

You know [another ZANU-PF base commander] had his young brother beaten in Ward 7 and you tell me that people were not possessed?'[11]

This horror at the intimacy of the violence was widespread. Gerald, a senior MDC official in Norton, explained, 'People were beaten up, houses were burnt and some people had to run away from their homes. And this was because of Zanu terror bases. These bases were not established by people from outside. It was our own friends, relatives and young who were in them. Up to now I still wonder at what happened.'[12] This 'wonder' marked the real struggle very many people had in trying to make sense of the violent behaviour of friends and relatives with whom they had grown up and lived alongside. It marked out 2008 as a moment in which people became unknowable to one another, and explanations (where they were proffered—some maintained these things could not be explained at all) drew on ideas of madness, possession, and the reduction of social beings to an animal status. For some these acts were unforgivable and resulted in a refusal, long after the June violence, even to greet the ZANU-PF members involved.[13] Where victims of violence in the bases interacted with their former tormenters, they often did so only at the price of constantly reminding them of their cruel deeds, especially if they were asking for a favour or a beer, so as to shame and humiliate them and to underline how little they had gained from their willingness to use violence on behalf of ZANU-PF. One man, an ex-soldier who had been beaten in the bases by his neighbours, made it a point to train himself physically so he could intimidate them. In other cases, the madness of those who had used violence was attributed to witchcraft used by their victims—people less restrained than Nathan had been. One such notorious case involved a ZANU-PF-supporting woman who worked at the town council and had established a reputation for cruelly beating MDC women. She was widely rumoured to have gone mad in early 2010 due to her victims' use of witchcraft, and was thereafter commonly found wandering around a Ngoni shopping centre.[14]

Understandings of the meaning of acts of violence in Norton in 2008 powerfully shaped their consequences for individuals and for social relations. As these acts were understood to abrogate highly valued social norms among neighbours and kin they were rendered inexplicable and unforgivable in varied ways, leaving in their wake profound obstacles to the reconstitution of social relations, expressed in the mediums of ostracism, witchcraft, madness, humiliation, and the constant retelling of tales of cruelty in daily interactions. If social norms and their rupture shaped the consequences of this violence, so too did the imbrications of political violence and economic relations.

Vulnerability, Patronage and Politics

For the MDC in Norton, the provision of material and other forms of support demonstrated the party's ability to care for its own in the face of arrests and violence. Such acts were important to its identity and capacity. In order to play this role, the MDC relied on mobilising both individuals and a wide civic network so as to gain access to funds, legal and medical expertise and other resources. In 2008, the combination of violence and the contraction of economic opportunity placed such relations in jeopardy and rendered MDC activists acutely vulnerable. ZANU-PF's use of material resources was different, but equally central to its identity and capacity. It relied on the state's assets and the state's ability to control assets, and it deployed its resources to encourage and to coerce performances of loyalty and—crucially—to mobilise violence. ZANU-PF's use of state resources for political purposes is of course well known. Our point here is to emphasise the way in which such practices were woven into the organisation of violence, creating particular kinds of incentives, expectations and relationships.[15]

A key source of jobs and livelihoods in Norton in the late 2000s was the fishing industry.[16] It had grown in importance as other industries—Cone Textiles, Hunyani Pulp and Paper Industry, a metal manufacturing company called Bestobell, the timber processing plant Wilgro Sawmills—went into decline in the 1990s and 2000s. The number of fisheries mushroomed from two to over 16 after 2005. These cooperative-run enterprises relied on two nearby dams, Darwendale/Manyame and Lake Chivero. Many people from Norton made their living either as members of the cooperatives or by purchasing fish from them for resale.[17] From the mid-2000s, the award of licences to cooperatives (a process officially in the hands of the Department of National Parks and Wildlife Management) came increasingly under partisan control as senior ZANU-PF leaders sought to reward ZANU-PF youths for their loyalty and 'activism', defined as a willingness to engage in political violence. Through publicly performing their loyalty in this way, some youths gained much coveted direct access to cooperative membership. Those not lucky enough to receive licences were given preference in buying fish from the cooperatives. MDC members were increasingly excluded from both the cooperatives and from buying fish for resale.

ZANU-PF forged a link between coercive politics and access to resources in other spheres too. Important among them was access to local market stalls. Before 2008, ZANU-PF attempts to exert control over market stalls resulted in the eviction of some traders and violent conflicts. In the period of extreme violence in 2008, ZANU-PF youths intervened far more directly, 'vetting' stall-holders for their loyalty, and leaving them with the options of losing their livelihoods, physically defending themselves from attack, or publicly expressing their support for ZANU-PF. Most opted for the latter; physical battles could not be won in 2008 and the economic costs of losing a stall might threaten an extended family's very survival. The extreme food shortages and high food prices of these years made another resource crucial to survival—the Grain Marketing Board (GMB) depot. Norton is home to Zimbabwe's second largest depot. In the late 2000s, ZANU-PF developed a practice of granting local 'cooperatives' the right to procure maize from the depot and mill it for sale. Those actively aligned to ZANU-PF were given privileged access. A final significant source of patronage was the town council: access to jobs and other resources such as vehicles also increasingly required demonstrating support for the ruling party.

Belonging to ZANU-PF or simply feigning support for it became a matter of survival for many ordinary people as forging livelihoods beyond ZANU-PF's grasp became more and more difficult. In 2008, the newly arrived 'colonel' made a point of loudly bragging about his access to the GMB stores and other resources, thereby marking himself out as a political patron, willing to build relations with clients on the back of access to state resources and violence.

The MDC's attempts to protect its support and its activists had to draw on other resources. Some of the few remaining privately owned industrial concerns in Norton were crucial to particular groups of MDC activists who had started out in the trade union movement; but many MDC youths worked outside state-controlled networks and formal employment, eking out a living in the increasingly precarious informal sector, selling bread or cell-phone airtime, illegally working as fish-mongers, and making a living as itinerant carpenters or cross-border traders.[18] The MDC, both locally and from its national headquarters in Harare, and with the help of a network of sympathetic civic organisations, made great efforts to support activists when they were injured, arrested or otherwise in need (see Alexander, 2010). Activists were none the less extremely vulnerable in 2008 owing to the combination of intensifying political violence and the rapidly deteriorating and politicised economy.

This vulnerability constituted a threat to the MDC's capacity to sustain the bonds of obligation and care that were essential to its identity and organisational capacity. MDC leaders in Norton felt responsible for the hardships suffered particularly by the youth, who bore the brunt of ZANU-PF violence. After the arrest of a large number of MDC youth following the attack on the ZANU-PF bases in mid-June 2008, Gerald explained:

We were devastated. As a party and as individuals. These are not only active and committed members of the party but also our young brothers. You know MDC members in Norton are a close knit community. We decided as a District to pool our resources together to assist them. The unfortunate thing was that at the time most of our people had been displaced and some had gone into hiding so we were a bit handicapped in terms of how we could collectively assist the boys. We looked for lawyers for them and made sure that they got food and that their families were catered for. We tried to liaise with the police officers who were sympathetic to our cause, and they were many by the way, but they had limited options and powers in terms of how they could assist us.[19] We did the best we could as a party but the ZANU-PF machinery at the time was vicious and remember we also feared for our lives and this meant that our movements and hence the ability to mobilise was severely handicapped.[20]

Gerald emphasised the role of material exchanges as expressions of solidarity, sacrifice and kinship: the MDC youth were his 'young brothers'. Failure in maintaining these bonds was keenly felt.

In 2008, the price of opposition in Norton was paid not only in monetary forms, but also in the currency of health, relationships and social standing. When we asked three young male MDC activists what effects political violence had had on their lives, they focused on the 'bleakness' of their futures and their personal relationships. These three young men had suffered violent attacks, and had spent more than a month in the police cells in Norton and in Harare Remand Prison from mid-June 2008 on charges of involvement in the attacks on the bases. In prison, they suffered from lack of food, despite the support of the MDC, which placed them in a far better position than many other prisoners, and were subjected to the disease-ridden, overcrowded conditions and constant threats of physical and sexual abuse typical of prisons in this period (Alexander, 2009). When we interviewed them in early 2009, they were out on bail, and were required to report to the police station in Norton every Friday and to the court in Harare every two weeks.

The devastating effect of these experiences emerged in its many dimensions as they exchanged thoughts on their lives:

Maxwell: This is affecting us seriously. We don't have a plan to work for ourselves. We see our future as bleak ... The bail conditions restrict our movement. We have to report every Friday at Norton police station. Thomas is a freelance carpenter and he works around the country, but now he has to work just in Norton, because of having to report to the police and because of the money needed for appearing in court. Thomas's business is affected and that affects the rest of us. He used to sub-contract to us and now he can't so it has terrible effects on our financial situation.

Benjamin: Since 27 June my business [as a mobile bread seller] has been disrupted and I lost capital because of the transport fees to appear in court. We're now failing to take care of family. We're being punished ...

Maxwell: For me the pain is physical. Before [going to prison] I enjoyed sports, running, but when I try to jog I lose breath. I have pain in the chest. My strength is drastically reduced. I think it's because of the dirty blankets [in the cells].

Thomas: I developed an irritation on the skin—spots. And psychologically I have not dealt with the loss of income. My business collapsed. It took me a long time to find my footing again.

Benjamin: For me there were three effects. On the political front, as a youth leader, some of the youth lost their initiative and drive. Morale was affected. And it's had a huge impact on my health. When it's hot I get skin irritations. I'm always used to hard work but now I'm limited in how hard I can work. I can't work at the same level ...

Maxwell: After we were released I went home to find I was homeless. We were renting this place and my property had been destroyed—the bed broken, clothes burnt—by ZANU-PF youth. My wife went back to her parents. I couldn't find a place to stay. People were afraid to let me stay, that their house would be destroyed. So I had to search for accommodation and food—that was one of the most traumatic experiences of the whole time ...

Benjamin: I was supposed to have married a specific girl, but I lost her when I was in jail and I'm trying to deal with that up to now.

Maxwell: The biggest problem I have ... is I lost property and my birth certificate and national ID and school certificate and passport. I haven't recovered from that. Such things are so difficult to acquire now.

Thomas: I lost my carpentry tools. Some were taken to relatives. I haven't been able to find them all.

Maxwell: The harassment also overlapped with my mother. She was taken to the base and made to cook food for three days and harassed and made to shout slogans and to swear she would put rat poison in my food when I came home. We have *ngozi* [a type of avenging spirit]—if your mother is harassed on your behalf it hangs on you and affects your future.[21]

Maxwell was required to make a payment (*kuripa*) to his mother's relatives to be rid of these terrible consequences, but could not afford to do so. Maxwell's case had echoes in others where the costs of opposition political activism weighed heavily on family members. Wives and children were often rendered vulnerable. Maxwell's wife had found herself not only in danger but also homeless and without an income. She had gone back to her parents as a result. Benjamin had lost his fiancée and remained broken-hearted. Others told similar stories of family losses, division and anger. Nathan explained that his mother blamed his elder brother, a senior MDC leader, for the violence he had suffered in the base and his subsequent arrest.[22]

For Mary, the costs of her husband Christopher's MDC activism had been devastating. She explained how she had fled to her husband's parents in Domboshava in June, in fear for her children. She had returned when Christopher was arrested. 'I cried endlessly. I thought he was going to be killed ... I cursed God for getting us into trouble.' Mary was helped by Norton MDC leaders with money to buy food to take to her husband at the police station each day and to feed her family. She spoke to Christopher about family and her welfare, 'but we really didn't say much', Mary explained, 'I was crying and he was crying' and they were always watched by a policeman.[23] The situation worsened when Christopher was moved to Harare Remand Prison, as Mary explained:

It was very difficult. We heard stories of how MDC people were being killed and kidnapped and how those who were being sent to jail were not going to come out. I also had to make plans to go and see him there and I could not manage to do so in the first week. I [then] moved to Mbare [a township in Harare] to my sister's house and would walk to remand prison almost every day. Fortunately we got food from Harvest House [the MDC headquarters in Harare] which we could eat whilst waiting to see him. But I could not continue staying in Mbare because my sister only uses 2 rooms and she has a family. I went back to Norton and had to depend on Musumbu [the MP] and other MDC people for news about their welfare and case. I also started to have problems at the place we used to stay because they were no longer comfortable about staying with MDC people. And you can imagine, the person who owns the house is my *Maiguru* [older sister to Mary's mother] and she supports ZANU-PF. She was now saying that she had always told [Christopher] not to support MDC, and now look what it has gotten him into. She was defending herself saying she did not want her house to be burnt so she could not have us continue staying at her place. We had to move and I had no money to do so. My property ended up spending weeks outside or I had to ask from friends to keep it for me. I was also supposed to feed the family and how was I going to do that with no money in the pocket?[24]

Although Christopher continued to receive food from the MDC while in remand prison, support for his wife dried up as arrests and harassment of MDC supporters who were Christopher's friends prevented them from providing food and money and the Norton MDC's funds ran low.

The consequences of political violence thus reverberated through people's lives and relationships in and after 2008. They stretched the bonds built through material care by the MDC; they endangered, divided and impoverished families and broke romantic relationships; they destroyed livelihoods, and robbed people of their property and papers and homes; they weakened bodies; and they caused spiritual harm. The range of these consequences flowed not just from the individual acts of violence themselves, but from the ways in which they interacted with productive, material and social relations in Norton and within and between ZANU-PF and the MDC.

Violence and Politics after the Inclusive Government

When we asked male MDC activists how their losses had affected their commitment to the MDC, they without exception said it had strengthened their passion and loyalty.[25] When we asked them what should be done with perpetrators of violence, they unanimously said they should be prosecuted in the courts. As Gerald put it, 'Those who committed crimes should be answerable for their crimes—simple'.[26] Such statements were important indications of intent and expectation; but they did not tell the whole story of political discourse among MDC supporters after the installation of the Inclusive Government. In 2009 and after, a new and uncomfortable set of stories and debates emerged among MDC stalwarts and their at times less enthusiastic kin. These hinged on the nature of debt and obligation now that the MDC was no longer an opposition movement but held government office and had access to state institutions and resources.

In this new context, rumours of corruption and broken bonds peppered stories of dashed expectations. Mary, who is not herself an active MDC supporter, explained:

I have suffered enough for this party and I wish Christopher [her husband] could see it. Right now I don't even know where I am going to get money to pay rent for the end of this month. I sell fish but the money is not enough to keep us and the family. We hear there has been food and money, which has been donated to us from some MDC senior members but the food does not get to us. Musumbu [the MP] is busy spending the money. That is very unfair, to suffer so that some people can feed their families using your name. I have always told Christopher this and he doesn't listen. Until when are we going to suffer for the party so that some people can enjoy? Right now there has been talk about starting a fishery for us and it has been 6 months and nothing has materialised ... Even MDC is just as corrupt as Zanu. Especially Musumbu. He does not care about the people who fought to have him voted into power and I think he needs to be told that he won't get our votes next time if he continues to do that ... [The party] should at least have given them money for projects. They know they are not employed and are people who worked very hard for MDC in Norton but they leave them to suffer. Christopher has always been a person who survives from using his hands. But his tools and everything was either lost or destroyed during our suffering, so he has nowhere to start from.

Mary swore she would never vote for any party, but she despaired of changing her husband's views: 'It's pointless to do that because he won't listen. [He] loves MDC and I don't even know why. He may complain, and he may tell you that they have let him down but he will always love that party. Maybe he sees what he gets from being a member.'[27]

Despite his continued devotion to the MDC, Christopher's views were not in fact so different from those of his wife. He also believed that the institution of the Inclusive Government and the access it promised to resources and employment meant that the MDC should take care of those—such as himself—who had suffered most in the violence of 2008. He felt deeply aggrieved by what he saw as the Norton MDC MP's corruption and betrayal of his obligations, a view fuelled by rumours of goods being siphoned off and access to patrons denied:

When we were prisoners, we knew we were prisoners and we could do nothing but now we are more imprisoned because of the MP. Because even [the MDC MP for Marondera] who wants to help us can not do so because when we go to our MP he simply says that things are difficult but we then hear rumours that he actually took stuff that was meant for us to his rural area ... [W]e gave him an avenue that he now uses to get commodities for himself. I think the MP is the biggest problem because when we go to him with ideas on how he can help us he simply uses them to his benefit. We even told him that as an MP, why don't you try to find us jobs in the town council since it is now being run by MDC but all he says is that the council is facing a lot of problems. So where can we work? Why then don't you get us jobs in other companies? But nothing materialises. You actually hear that another person who never went through what we did has gotten a job or has benefited ... If only he could just take food and the stuff that is meant for us and use it for himself but then give us jobs so we could earn a few dollars, that could be better. But right now we are stuck.

These narratives of betrayed obligations contrasted starkly with the solidarity of the pre-Inclusive Government period when the MDC was seen by activists, if not always by their families, to be helping to the best of its ability. They are also stories of blocked progress: Christopher is 'stuck', and he was even taunted by some for having foolishly suffered for nothing—'people tell you hurtful things like "you were just arrested and you did not gain anything from it and some people are the ones who are benefiting instead of you." So you see that person will just add to your misery ...' Christopher blamed his misery and inability to progress not on ZANU-PF but on the MDC, and specifically his MP: 'He is supposed to be there for us, representing us, but he is the one who is making life difficult for us.'[28]

This political discourse was born of the real existential crises that so many young MDC men faced in the aftermath of the 2008 violence. It marked a shift to a language of patronage in which material obligations were no longer constructed in terms of kinship, sacrifice and solidarity among opposition party members, but as debt owed for suffering now payable by a party in power.

For ZANU-PF, neither the language of patronage nor access to state office and resources were new, but there were also angry ructions within the party after the formation of the Inclusive Government. We interviewed very few, and mostly junior, ZANU-PF members, but those we did speak to harboured feelings of bitterness. Two ZANU-PF youths, Maurice and Samuel, both of whom worked maintaining irrigation equipment on a farm near Norton, explained that they had fallen out with Norton's ZANU-PF hierarchy. They had been arrested in mid-August 2008 on charges of rape and causing grievous bodily harm in the bases during June. Both were out on bail. They claimed they were innocent and had been made scapegoats by the more senior ZANU-PF men and women who had been involved in the crimes, notably Norton's youth chairman and his wife. Samuel explained that he believed they had been targeted because they were seen as backward farm-workers and so dispensable, in contrast to the more favoured 'town boys' of ZANU-PF. As proof of their victimisation, the two men said they had been struck off the membership list of a recently created fishing cooperative by the district youth chairman's wife. Maurice asked that a message be passed on to the youth chairman: if he continued to behave in this way, Maurice would resort to the use of witchcraft against him.[29] Another group of three ZANU-PF supporters we talked to were less willing to criticise openly the party leadership, but they also noted at length their reduced circumstances and the failure of the party to support them, either when they had been imprisoned in an earlier incident or in their current circumstances. One contrasted the support given to MDC activists with their own situation, in which ZANU-PF did nothing to help them. He whispered at the end of the interview that he felt 'betrayed'.[30]

Some ZANU-PF members at least have been left in an awkward place. On the one hand, as we have seen, ZANU-PF youth and others who had been prominently involved in violence in 2008 often faced extremely difficult relations with the neighbours and kin they had once tormented. On the other hand, senior ZANU-PF leaders in Norton who had lost their offices—though not necessarily their access to state resources—no longer felt they 'owed' them the wages of violence or indeed anything at all.[31] This does not, of course, mean that such men cannot be mobilised again and on exactly the same basis, as indeed they have been.

Conclusion

The narratives of obligation and blame created by histories of political violence in Norton have had multiple—and shifting—effects on social relations among kin and neighbours, and on political relations between them and their leaders. The violence of 2008 was organised from the centre and very efficiently targeted opposition members, but it was interpreted through the prism of Norton's social norms, and took on meaning as a result of being seen as an almost inexplicable moment of rupture. This view powerfully shaped its ongoing consequences for social relations, played out in stories about madness and witchcraft and in retaliatory humiliations and exclusions. The high costs of violence for opposition members—with implications for so many aspects of their lives and relationships—were born of the links between coercive politics and people's livelihoods. The MDC's ability to care for its own was undermined and its members' vulnerability greatly exacerbated, with terrible and far from resolved consequences. ZANU-PF's backers were drawn—voluntarily and not—into an exchange of violence for material reward, orchestrated with military ruthlessness, though often with no lasting benefits, and with real costs, for the rank and file. For both parties, the Inclusive Government brought new challenges, but they were perhaps most difficult for the MDC whose leaders found their bonds with followers, once constructed as kin, had been converted into a currency of patronage payable for suffering endured. In the era of the Inclusive Government, they struggled—unconvincingly in the eyes of many of their supporters—to respond.

Notes

1. ZANU-PF is the Zimbabwe African National Union–Patriotic Front, the party that has ruled Zimbabwe since independence. Veterans of Zimbabwe's liberation war formed an alliance with the ruling party in 1997 and were prominent in the occupation of white-owned farms and the organisation of violence after 2000. Youth militias were formed after 2000 by ZANU-PF and have been used extensively in electoral and other political violence.
2. The human rights reporting on Zimbabwe is voluminous and rigorous. For some of the best reporting by Zimbabwe-based organisations, see Solidarity Peace Trust (2008a, b), and for a consideration of the organisation of political violence in Zimbabwe in 2008, see Alexander and Tendi (2008).
3. For example, interview, Edgar, MDC activist, Norton, 23 February 2010.
4. Interview, Benjamin, MDC activist, Harare, 21 February 2009.
5. The term 'youth' in this context refers to a political category—party youth may be young, but many youth leaders on both sides were in their 30s and 40s.
6. Interview, Garfield, Norton, 23 February 2010.
7. Interviews, Christopher, Norton, May 2009; Benjamin, Maxwell and Thomas, Harare, 21 February 2009; Gerald, Norton, May 2009, all of whom are MDC activists or leaders.
8. Nathan's parents and Marcus's parents worked as cooks in the same school.
9. Interview, Nathan, Norton, 17 May 2009.
10. Interview, Nathan, Norton, 23 May 2009.
11. Interview, Nathan, Norton, 23 May 2009.
12. Interview, Gerald, Norton, May 2009.
13. Interview, Aaron, MDC activist, Norton, 26 May 2009.
14. Informal discussions and observations by Kudakwashe Chitofiri in Norton, March 2010.
15. Food distribution, for example, has notoriously been closely controlled by ZANU-PF in order to reward its supporters and punish opposition members. See e.g. Human Rights Watch (2003).
16. Information on the Norton economy and its political uses compiled by Kudakwashe Chitofiri on the basis of informal discussion and observation.
17. Cooperatives average about 16 members and employ about 30 workers each. The numbers involved in the buying and selling of fish are much larger.
18. Economic pressures did not of course affect only MDC youths. See Jones (2010) for a fascinating discussion of the livelihoods of young men since 2000 in the city of Chitungwiza.
19. Many MDC activists interviewed noted the existence of sympathetic police, who gave warnings and helped people who had been arrested in a variety of ways, but all also stressed that in June 2008 the police feared being labelled as sympathetic to the MDC and were themselves tightly policed by particular departments—the Criminal Investigation Department and Law and Order—as well as by war veterans in the police. For example, interview, Nathan, MDC activist, Norton, 17 May 2009.
20. Interview, Gerald, Norton, May 2009.
21. Interview, Benjamin, Maxwell and Thomas, Harare, 21 February 2009.

22. Interview, Nathan, Norton, 17 May 2009.
23. Interview, Mary, Norton, May 2009.
24. Interview, Mary, Norton, May 2009.
25. For example, interviews, Benjamin, Maxwell and Thomas, Harare, 21 February 2009; Nathan, Norton, 23 May 2009.
26. Interview, Gerald, Norton, May 2009.
27. Interview, Mary, Norton, May 2009.
28. Interview, Christopher, Norton, May 2009.
29. Interview, Maurice and Samuel, ZANU-PF youth, Norton, 24 May 2009.
30. Interview, James, Marcus and Jasper, ZANU-PF youth, Harare, 24 February 2009.
31. Compare with accounts of and by other disgruntled ZANU-PF members in Eppel (2009, p. 971) and Alexander (2010).

References

Alexander, J. (2009) Death and disease in Zimbabwe's prisons, *The Lancet*, 373(21), pp. 995–996.

Alexander, J. (2010) The political imaginaries and social lives of political prisoners in post-2000 Zimbabwe, *Journal of Southern African Studies*, 36(2), pp. 483–503.

Alexander, J. and Tendi, B.-M. (2008) La violence et les urnes: le Zimbabwe en 2008, *Politique Africaine*, 111, pp. 111–129.

Cheeseman, N. and Tendi, B.-M. (2010) Power-sharing in comparative perspective: the dynamics of 'unity government' in Kenya and Zimbabwe, *Journal of Modern African Studies*, 48, pp. 203–229.

Eppel, S. (2009) A tale of three dinner plates: truth and the challenges of human rights research in Zimbabwe, *Journal of Southern African Studies*, 35(4), pp. 966–976.

Human Rights Watch (2003) *Not Eligible: The Politicization of Food in Zimbabwe* (New York: Human Rights Watch).

Jones, J. (2010) 'Nothing is straight in Zimbabwe': the rise of the kukiya-kiya economy, 2000–2008, *Journal of Southern African Studies*, 36(2), pp. 285–299.

Solidarity Peace Trust (2008a) *Desperately Seeking Sanity: What Prospects for a New Beginning in Zimbabwe?* (Johannesburg: Solidarity Peace Trust).

Solidarity Peace Trust (2008b) *Punishing Dissent, Silencing Citizens: The Zimbabwe Elections 2008* (Johannesburg: Solidarity Peace Trust).

Diasporic Repositioning and the Politics of Re-engagement: Developmentalising Zimbabwe's Diaspora?

JOANN McGREGOR* AND DOMINIC PASURA**
*Migration Research Unit, University College London, London, UK
**School of Health and Human Sciences Research, University of Huddersfield, Huddersfield, UK

ABSTRACT *The power-sharing agreement in Zimbabwe has ushered in a period of engagement between the diaspora and homeland government, marking a distinct change from the hostility that characterised relations over previous years. This article discusses the politics of this repositioning and the character of the new diasporic organisations formed in the wake of the Global Political Agreement to take forward agendas of development and reconstruction at home. It argues that these new diasporic organisations have tried to create non-partisan platforms for engagement, have an elite social base, and connect responsibilities for development at home with the desire for formal political rights. Despite an apparent convergence of interest around development and reconstruction on the part of an array of diaspora groups, as well as the Zimbabwean and British governments, there are, nonetheless, tensions among these actors that this article seeks to reveal. It argues that a key issue shaping conversations over engagement is the divergence of interest within the diaspora between those with and without security in their states of residence. This divide is likely to become more salient in the context of a large-scale return programme, especially if there is ongoing uncertainty in Zimbabwe and if repatriation is conceived as a final one-way movement rather than as part of an ongoing circulation in which people may choose to maintain transnational lives. This discussion of the Zimbabwean case thus contributes to broader debates over the tensions that characterise policies of 'diaspora engagement'.*

Introduction

On 20 June 2009, Morgan Tsvangirai addressed an audience of 1000 Zimbabweans in London's Southwark Cathedral, appealing for them to 'come home'. The crowd was optimistic and excited. Despite increasing concern over the lack of progress in key areas during the first four months of power-sharing, 16 diasporic associations had issued an advance statement welcoming formal engagement and pointing to the diaspora's future role in reconstruction and development in Zimbabwe. Unlike Tsvangirai's previous visits in his capacity as the Movement for Democratic Change (MDC) leader, where he had addressed meetings of party supporters, this was different—he was touring as Prime Minister and his addresses were quite explicitly to all Zimbabweans. The London address was part of a tour of Europe, the United Kingdom and the United States, in which the aim was both to make contact with the diaspora and to meet with Western politicians and officials to raise funds for the cash-strapped new unity government.

Yet the optimism that preceded the event, which was also evident at the outset of the address, quickly faded. When Tsvangirai called for the diaspora to return and claimed that the situation in Zimbabwe was one of 'peace and stability', he was shouted down with chants of 'Mugabe must go' and calls for politicians' children to return first, while the MDC slogan 'chinja [change]' was used to mock his claims. Clearly shocked, Tsvangirai left the pulpit and abandoned his speech. Returning after a few minutes, he instead took questions, but the organisers of the event struggled to restore order as the disruption continued.[1]

Notwithstanding this confusion, the address marked a watershed in relations between the Zimbabwean government and its diaspora. It ignited heated debate, a flurry of conferences and helped consolidate new diaspora organisations orientated towards reconstruction at home. The contrast with diasporic activity over previous years was stark. Until the signing of the Global Political Agreement (GPA) between the ruling Zimbabwe African National Union-Patriotic Front (ZANU-PF) and the two MDC opposition parties, which laid the basis for the Government of National Unity (GNU) in February 2009, relationships between the Zimbabwe government and the diaspora were notably hostile. Diasporic politics had been dominated by anti-ZANU-PF activity: a network of MDC branches (formalised into external MDC assemblies in 2006) had worked together with overseas offices of Zimbabwean civics and diaspora community associations to raise the profile of ZANU-PF human rights abuses and to pursue the goal of political transition at home (Raftopoulos, 2006; McGregor, 2009, 2010; Pasura, 2008, 2010). At the same time Mugabe and ZANU-PF had consistently cast diasporans as disloyal and traitorous puppets of British and Western imperial interests. In this highly politicised context and as the Zimbabwe economy imploded, diaspora/homeland relations were not primarily concerned with development. Attempts by ZANU-PF to court diasporic finance through policies of diaspora engagement fashionable with governments and Western donors had been dismal failures.

Tsvangirai's visit thus heralded the advent of a new era of engagement, typified by new types of diasporic performance, staged by a new cast of actors. The interests of these new actors converged with those of the Prime Minister's Office in Zimbabwe, as it began to reach out to Zimbabweans abroad, trying to capitalise on their financial potential and skills. In contrast to the politicised rhetoric of the previous decade, the new initiatives have been cast overwhelmingly in terms of development discourse, and are dominated by debates over financial investment and harnessing professional expertise for reconstruction. All players involved were keen to move away from divisive party politics, and to come up with new, explicitly non-partisan frameworks. Although these new initiatives converge in their desire to depoliticise the diaspora, at the same time they have thrown into the spotlight conflicting interests—within diasporic communities, between diasporas and homeland and hosting governments, and between different arms of government and state.

This article explores this new politics of diaspora engagement, and its re-focus around development, drawing on web sources and participant observation of these processes in the British context. We argue that the shift towards development discourse should be seen not as de-politicisation but rather as a reconfiguration and repositioning, as the diasporic organisations taking the agenda forward compete to raise their profile and jostle to be the prime point of contact representing 'the diaspora' to governments. Our aim in describing this politics in the Zimbabwean context is to reveal some of the tensions within policy discourses of diaspora engagement.

An emerging literature has begun to critique some of the assumptions that can underpin policy-makers' recent 'remittance euphoria' and deflate its more exaggerated claims (De Haas, 2005; Faist, 2008). Bakewell (2008a, b) argues that policies of diaspora engagement overemphasise the role and interests of skilled wealthy migrants in Western countries, and tend to ignore displaced people within Africa and non-elites at home. Yet regionally based migrants can be more important as proximity allows for a more intimate ongoing relationship with home, and financial and material flows can exceed those from further afield (Mercer *et al.*, 2008). Other authors point out that diaspora engagement policies can also misrepresent the lives and interests of the majority of migrants within Western countries: Datta *et al.* (2007) show that most remittance-senders struggle to make ends meet through low-paid work, and question the assumption that the burden of development should also fall on their shoulders, while Orozco (2008) casts diaspora remittances simply as foreign savings, and sees no reason why governments should have any claim on them. Brinkerhoff (2010) argues that diasporic communities do not want to be seen simply as a source of money, but desire recognition as citizens, while homeland governments prefer to tap their wealth but limit political engagement. She also raises the possibility of diasporic organisations being instrumentalised by Western governments in similar ways to non-governmental organisations (NGOs) within dominant neo-liberal frameworks (Brinkerhoff, 2010). Indeed, the interests of governments of origin and residence can converge in so far as neither likes to think of diasporic communities as comprised of citizens with political interests in two countries: Western hosting governments have cast diaspora transnational ties as a threat to integration, whereas homeland governments like to emphasise only the 'homeland' dimensions of diasporic identity, and both prefer to stress unthreatening developmental agendas over diasporas' political potential (Brinkerhoff, 2010). A further source of tension is apparent when Western hosting governments have linked the agenda of diaspora engagement to programmes of return. Black and Gent (2006, p. 15) challenge governments' conceptualisation of repatriation as a final, one-way move and suggest that 'continued mobility after an initial return—including circulation and the development of a "transnational lifestyle"—may be more "sustainable" than a single and definitive return to the refugees' place of origin'.

To shed further light on potentially conflicting interests in the Zimbabwean case, we begin by exploring initiatives emanating from the Government of Zimbabwe

(GoZ) and the controversy that followed Tsvangirai's London address described at the outset. We then turn to initiatives coming from the diaspora, analysing the new actors and associations that have arisen in the United Kingdom in the context of British government policy.

Wooing the Diaspora: Morgan Tsvangirai's Outreach

The disruption of Tsvangirai's London address was significant in many ways—for the light it shed on social cleavages within the diaspora, its impact on subsequent MDC and GoZ outreach policies, and for the insight it gave into how problems of power-sharing could affect the MDC's international support base. As such, it is worth revisiting the aftermath of the event in more detail.

Within the diaspora in Britain, the immediate response to Tsvangirai's humiliating treatment was sharply polarised. Many Zimbabweans were 'appalled' at the 'unAfrican' treatment their Prime Minister had received (Gonda, 2009). Yet critics of power-sharing felt Tsvangirai risked losing his traditional supporters through lack of honesty about the problems involved, and because it gave the British government reason not to grant Zimbabweans asylum and to resume enforced returns. These opinions were voiced, respectively, by organisations representing professionals with security in Britain on the one hand, and those representing asylum seekers on the other.

Speaking for the organisations keen to engage, the Zimbabwe Diaspora Development Interface (ZDDI), founded by professionals in 2008, released a public statement welcoming the call for Zimbabweans in the United Kingdom to consider going back home and deeply regretting 'the appalling disruptive behaviour by a special interest group' (Gonda, 2009). The ZDDI argued that the disruption reflected the privileging of 'narrow' individual asylum interests over and above the interests of the homeland. They also cast the disruption as orchestrated and blamed the leadership of two long-standing diasporic associations—the Vigil (maintained by a team of activists outside Zimbabwe House, London, who have demonstrated against Mugabe/ZANU-PF every Saturday since 2002 and whose supporters are mainly asylum-seekers) and Restoration of Human Rights (ROHR), a human rights organisation led by ex-MDC-UK leader Ephraim Tapa, whose membership is also primarily asylum-seekers. The Vigil and ROHR for their part vigorously denied organising the disruption, casting the event as 'spontaneous' and a 'reflection of feeling within the diaspora' (Gonda, 2009), pointing to mixed progress within the country and insecurity among asylum-seekers that deportations would follow: 'The issue is that Zimbabwe is still not safe to return for those who fled persecution and are in need of international protection. ROHR Zimbabwe and the Zimbabwe Vigil does not apologise to anyone for our principled stance that "Mugabe Must Go", our demand for democracy and justice, respect for the rule of law and the Restoration of Human Rights' (ROHR, 2009).

The politics of blame that unfolded thus revealed a key cleavage within the diaspora and divergent interests between professionals with legal status in Britain, who were unthreatened by calls to return, and asylum-seekers who feared being forced back. It also indicated an unresolved problem of who should represent 'the diaspora' and its range of views. Asylum-seekers' anxieties appeared to be fulfilled by the UK Border Agency (UKBA) response, which was to announce the intention to change returns policy, to scale up the package offered to voluntary returnees and to 'move towards' reversing the moratorium on deportations to Zimbabwe (Home Office, 2009; Woolas, 2009). Zimbabwean asylum claims in Britain had surged over the course of 2009, with 5,420 new claims in the year bringing the total number of Zimbabwean claims up to 29,800, and topping the list of nationalities seeking asylum for the second year running.[2] This was partly a direct response to the elevated violence of 2008 in Zimbabwe, and partly because the country guidance case 'RN' in the British Asylum and Immigration Tribunal in November 2008 encouraged people to come forward as it facilitated successful claims.[3] Most new asylum claims in this period were not people fleeing Zimbabwe directly, but those already in Britain.[4] The evident desire within UKBA to 'normalise' returns and bring down the asylum statistics, however, has been restrained by the unsteady progress within Zimbabwe, ongoing human rights abuses, and the hesitation among Western governments including the British government's Foreign and Commonwealth Office (FCO) to engage fully with the GoZ or remove sanctions on ZANU-PF members of it.

The rumpus over Tsvangirai's address also provoked a rethinking of outreach strategy on the part of the Prime Minister's Office, as visiting MDC ministers and other Zimbabwean speakers have subsequently been much more careful about what they say, often elaborating the view that the time is not right for Zimbabweans to return, even when addressing meetings where how to engage the diaspora and think about 'sustainable return' is the explicit agenda. When Minister of State Enterprises and Parastatals Gorden Moyo addressed a ZDDI conference on diaspora engagement in autumn 2009, for example, he was careful not to call the diaspora home. Rather, he said: 'There are opportunities in Zimbabwe for you, whether you choose to come home or to take advantage of them from abroad. But to make the most of these opportunities, you need to present professional, coordinated and comprehensive policy positions to help inform and guide the Government's policies towards engaging the Diaspora' (Musoro and Magaisa, 2009, p. 32). More straightforwardly, University of Zimbabwe Lecturer John Makumbe, addressing a similar event organised by a church umbrella group also in autumn 2009 (The Council of Zimbabwean Christian Leaders UK), argued bluntly that the diaspora should stay put: Zimbabweans at home needed their remittances, and the time to come home had not yet arrived.

The Prime Minister's Office also spearheaded a more formal process of migration policy development in partnership with the International Organisation for Migration (IOM). It is perhaps significant that this process began before the signing of the GPA. As early as 2007, GoZ/IOM workshops had formulated a new 'vision' for National Migration Management and Development ('to be an excellent model in the effective management and integration of migration for national development'; GoZ, 2010, p. 4); but this process was reinvigorated in 2008, as both the GPA itself and the Short Term Emergency Recovery Programme (STERP) acknowledged the role of the diaspora in reconstruction. Given the history of confrontational relations with ZANU-PF, outreach was facilitated by placing responsibility under the remit of the Prime Minister's Office. In April 2010, a Draft 'National Migration Management and Diaspora Policy', the product of two years' work between GoZ/IOM was circulated and diaspora stakeholders were invited to comment.

The final document is still under negotiation. In some ways the draft is unremarkable: it covers the range of issues one would expect—aiming to 'mitigate the flight of qualified professionals through skills retention programmes, formalise the export of labour to maximise the benefits to the economy, harness remittance revenues being contributed by the diaspora, create a conducive investment platform and strategies for the diaspora, provide a framework for diaspora engagement on socio-economic developments in the country . . .' (GoZ, 2010, p. 6). There has clearly been some effort not to overlook the interests of non-elite labour migrants within the region through policies to protect their rights, yet there are also some exaggerated claims about professionals. Although it is clear that the majority of the country's professional classes fled Zimbabwe's borders, the idea that 'the greater proportion' of the diaspora of four million people within SA, Botswana, Namibia, United Kingdom, United States, Australia and New Zealand 'represent the country's professionals and academics' is a clear overstatement (GoZ, 2010, p. 10). On the contentious question of citizenship the draft policy is contradictory, and the main section lacks text (GoZ, 2010, p. 10). The draft says in one place that policy on citizenship is to be guided by the process of consultation over the contested 'Kariba draft' of the constitution (which explicitly does not recognise dual citizenship), while stating elsewhere that a key strategy is 'to Amend the Constitution and Citizenship Act to allow for dual citizenship of Zimbabweans, extend voting rights to Zims in the diaspora'. While the draft makes clear migration and diaspora policy is only 'spearheaded' by the PM's office and will include a range of other ministries, it is also the case that there has been a notable silence on this issue from non-MDC ministers, and some of the key problems stalling the power-sharing agreement, such as ongoing ZANU-PF control of key ministries and the Reserve Bank and Western donors' unwillingness to work with ZANU-PF ministries, also hinder the unrolling of a formal diaspora engagement policy.

Drawn up initially by 'stakeholders within Zimbabwe', the draft is to be amended through input from consultations with the diaspora, so below we turn to how diaspora groups have articulated their interests.

Initiatives Emanating from the Diaspora

The plethora of new diaspora organisations that emerged immediately prior to the signing of the GPA in September 2008 and which have been consolidated thereafter advocate similar agendas of diaspora engagement. Here we focus primarily on the British context, but it is notable that in South Africa and the United States parallel initiatives exist, and there have been various efforts to join up diasporic efforts across continents. Some of the new players in the British context include the ZDDI, the Council of Zimbabwean Christian Leaders UK (CZCLUK), Zimbabwe Redevelopment Focus, Motherland Zimbabwe (MLZ), the Zimbabwe Gentlemen's Club (ZGC) and professional bodies such as the Zimbabwe Institute of Engineers UK.[5]

Despite their differences over calls to return with the longer established political and welfare groups, these new organisations share a national, Zimbabwean frame of reference (unlike the localised focus of diaspora development organisations common among other African groups, such as hometown associations; Mercer et al., 2008;

Page *et al.*, 2009). Below we explore four other features of the new development associations: their desire to be non-partisan, their social base in the diaspora elite, their desire to implicate themselves in Zimbabwean national reconstruction, and to link their developmental responsibilities at home to formal political rights.

The Creation of Non-partisan Spaces

The explicit aim to create a non-partisan platform for engagement is perhaps the most notable shift from the previous era of diaspora politics and its emphasis on confrontation and opposition to Mugabe. The new organisations have been keen to distance themselves from an alignment with either of the two MDCs or ZANU-PF. Over the period 2000–09, MDC exile politics had been fractious and factionalised to the point of provoking disillusion and disengagement among many former MDC members. Diaspora meetings had been characterised by fear and the suspicion of infiltration by Zimbabwean government intelligence operatives (CIO), by accusations of self-interest, corruption and money-making, by ethnic and racial tensions, by the acrimonious split between the two MDC factions, by a drift into support for Makoni in the 2008 elections, by an uneasy relationship with the MDC homeland party structures, and tensions between appointed and elected leaders (Magaisa, 2006; McGregor, 2009). The new organisations devoted to engagement and development were very keen to leave behind what many considered an uninspiring history of exile politics, and wanted to avoid the divisive polarisation between ZANU-PF and opposition as well as the factionalism between and within the two MDCs. Their aim was to create new spaces for constructive forms of engagement. As ZDDI elaborated at the time of their initiation: 'there is an absence of an over-arching platform among Zimbabwean groups in the UK where all competing interests can be openly and objectively debated without falling prey to party politics identities' (ZDDI, n.d.).

In seeking to create such a space, ZDDI cast itself as a 'non-partisan organisation which, from inception, has sought to provide a platform for dialogue, discussion and linkages between people and organisations from all walks of life with the common agenda of helping to reconstruct Zimbabwe' (Musoro and Magaisa, 2009, p. 8). The other new organisations had similar aims. Former MDC-UK officials, Gray Samakande and Godfrey Magwindiri, for example, established the Zimbabwe Redevelopment Focus as an opportunity for Zimbabweans in Britain to come together regardless of their political affiliation to explore ways of redeveloping the homeland (NZCN, 2009). The Council of Zimbabwean Christian Leaders UK has used its grounding in the Christian faith and church institutions to emphasise its non-partisanship, and to construct itself as capable of providing a credible and effective platform for engaging the diaspora in reconstructing the country. The 'platform will serve as a bridge and overcome obstacles posed by class, gender, colour, ethnic orientation or political affiliation' (CZCLUK, 2009). The series of meetings and conferences on the topic of engagement that have followed the signing of the GPA have involved the Zimbabwe embassy, as well as invitations to MDC Ministers and civic leaders. It is notable that invitations have not been extended to current ZANU-PF Ministers as organisers have been keen to show that non-partisanship does not mean sympathy with ZANU-PF.

The Primacy of the Diaspora's Educated Elite

These new diaspora development organisations are quite clearly comprised of the diaspora's most educated professional elites. ZDDI, for example, emerged out of a skills network formed in 2006. The cultural capital of their members has been an important aspect of their claims to authority in representing the diaspora, and gaining the confidence of homeland and hostland governments. The new associations can muster a wealth of qualifications, expertise and contacts, allowing them to cast themselves as professional and sophisticated, knowledgeable and trustworthy, with a combination of intimate understanding of the Zimbabwean context, familiarity with the business and social conventions of top-level world leaders and the capacity to mobilise the skills necessary for Zimbabwe's path to recovery. ZDDI calls itself a 'think-tank' in contrast, perhaps, to those who demonstrate on the streets, and seeks to provide 'a wider platform for the engagement of Zimbabweans abroad to harness intellectual capital, that is, new ideas and skills, experiences, networks, and financial resources for the development of Zimbabwe' (Musoro and Magaisa, 2009, p. 8). The Zimbabwe Gentlemen's Club combines its business and policy meetings with elite social events in the form of annual dinners and balls in exclusive London clubs. The elite character of these diaspora development organisations is evident from the profiles of core members: ZDDI's leadership has top-level expertise across its seven focus groups—Agriculture and Environment, Education, Finance and Economic Development, Health and Social Care, Industry and Technology, Media, Justice and Governance. The finance group, for example, comprises investment bankers, chartered accountants and investment analysts, while across the spectrum there is a multitude of PhDs, LLMs and other professional qualifications. Through their emphasis on the intellectual capital of their members and the construction of elite social worlds, these new developmental organisations have consciously distanced themselves from 'ordinary' diaspora members.

While the agenda of development and reconstruction is multi-faceted, and different organisations have different emphases, it is clear that generating finance and investment occupy a prominent place. Some of the new players, such as the Zimbabwe Gentlemen's Club, founded in April 2008, have placed this interest foremost, in aiming to generate wealth for members and to be 'influential on Zimbabwean matters' by 'facilitat[ing] an environment where respectable and successful Zimbabweans can engage in intellectual and apolitical exchange of ideas whilst promoting wealth generation amongst all its members and associates. The "Z" in the name stands for Zimbabwe and the "G" signifies Growth ... ZGClub has taken the on the lead role in being the independent voice of Zimbabwean Trade & Commerce Re-engagement within the Diaspora' (ZGClub, n.d.).

Claiming Responsibility for Homeland Reconstruction

The emergence of so many new diasporic organisations around the agenda of development and reconstruction clearly reflects the parallel surge of interest among Western donors and international organisations. Diasporic leaders want to be part of the action and desire to insert the voice of the diaspora within ongoing international and governmental debates. Since the late 1990s, the international community and Western governments have developed migration and development programmes, and have set up structures for diaspora consultation on selected policy issues (Department for International Development (DFID), 1997, 2007; Newland and Patrick, 2004; Brinkerhoff, 2008; World Bank, 2009). In 2009, DFID announced a budget of £20m managed by Comic Relief open to bids from diaspora organisations to participate in development at home, and also formalised diaspora volunteering schemes.[6] The African Diaspora Program of the World Bank, which focuses on diaspora policy formulation and implementation, finance, leveraging remittances and human capital for development (World Bank, 2009), held a consultative meeting with Zimbabwe diaspora groups in London on 4 May 2010. The IOM has also been active, working with diaspora organisations to document skills, draw up a database of diaspora associations and build partnerships, as, for example, with the Council for Assisting Refugee Academics (CARA) aiming to find ways to rebuild Zimbabwe's higher education sector. At the same time, the international community's funding for humanitarian programmes in Zimbabwe has soared since power-sharing, despite Western governments' decision to perpetuate targeted sanctions and withhold intergovernmental development aid until there is clearer progress on human rights and other issues. The British government, for its part, has combined maintaining the travel ban and asset freeze on a number of ZANU-PF individuals and companies with a huge increase in humanitarian spending: in 2008 and 2009, DFID's humanitarian expenditure in Zimbabwe amounted to £49m and £60m, the latter being the largest ever programme.[7]

This cautious re-engagement by Western donors and the strategising around large-scale future bi- and multilateral programmes of reconstruction have provided part of the stimulus for diaspora mobilisation. ZDDI explains: 'while most discussions about Zimbabwe hosted by UK-based research institutes continue to be informative, there is however a lack of ownership of the Zimbabwe debate by the Zimbabwean Diaspora, which should be aptly providing leadership on the subject'.[8] Professionals within the diaspora, feeling excluded from initial high-level governmental discussions about Zimbabwe's future, sought to insert themselves into ongoing conversations.

After Tsvangirai's visit to Britain, diaspora associations organised a flurry of conferences in London to try to fill this gap. ZDDI organised the largest of these events, focused on 'Investment, Development and Migration' and held at the University of East London on the 26 September 2009 with funding from the British government (Musoro and Magaisa, 2009). Over 250 participants attended to begin what ZDDI cast as a 'constructive conversation' on how the diaspora can assist reconstruction. The conference also provided an opportunity to 'develop a three-way direct dialogue' between the Zimbabwe GNU, the British government and the Zimbabwean diaspora (Musoro and Magaisa, 2009, p. 7). Senior GoZ ministers and officials attended, including Minister of State Gorden Moyo and Chief Executive Officers of the Zimbabwe Investment Authority and Zimbabwe Stock Exchange. On the part of the British government, FCO, DFID and UKBA participated. Gorden Moyo placed great emphasis on the diaspora's role:

> For us to rebuild our shattered economy and restore basic services and freedoms to the people we require support from the region, the international community

and, most importantly, you in the Diaspora. Your unique combination of home-grown knowledge and international skills and talents means that your current and potential contributions are vital if we are to succeed in building the Zimbabwe of tomorrow. (Musoro and Magaisa, 2009, p. 31)

Lazarus Muriritirwa, Director of Policy implementation at the PM's office (himself a returnee), described the PM office's 'fix the car while driving' approach, and pointed out that recovery so far has been due to efforts of Zimbabweans inside the country.[9] Emmanuel Munyukwi (CEO Zimbabwe Stock Exchange) echoed this plea for diaspora action, showing how the stock exchange had been rising rapidly, with markets being driven by non-Zimbabweans and assets being given away.[10] DFID for its part stated its willingness to engage with the diaspora, as long as this fitted in with Her Majesty's Government programmes and was also in harmony with those of GoZ.[11]

In the space of four days and also hosted within London's City, targeting the same audience, the Council of Zimbabwean Christian Leaders UK (CZCLUK) organised a similar (albeit less lavish) conference entitled 'Locating the Role of the Diaspora in Zimbabwe's Transitional Period' with funding from the Tear Fund UK, and speakers from Zimbabwe and the diaspora in the United States (John Makumbe from UZ and Ken Mufuka of the Zimbabwe Global Forum). CZCLUK (2009) described the conference as 'a significant step in providing an apolitical yet morally credible movement of Zimbabweans living abroad in fostering intelligent yet constructive debate, engagement and discourse that will give a definite voice to those in the Diaspora'. Although issues of finance and investment were included, the programme was diverse, with greater attention to issues of transitional justice and healing.[12]

There were also parallel events outside London. *Zimbabwe Investor Magazine* held a conference in Coventry in October 2009, which 'aimed at exploring business and investments opportunities in Zimbabwe as the country positions itself as one of the leading emerging economies, especially coming out of the global recession' (Chindodo, 2009). Gabriel Machinga, Zimbabwean High Commissioner, and the President of Employers Confederation of Zimbabwe, David Govere, were among the speakers. Chindodo (2009) explained the rationale of the conference:

Coming out of a period of political and economic turmoil, now known as 'the lost decade', Zimbabwe is looking to reconnect with the global economic family. The reconnection will involve the re-engagement of the country's Diaspora population, which constitute a significant portion of the most skilled labour force. The conference will explore ways which Zimbabwe's Diaspora population can best re-engage their homeland for development purposes.

Other initiatives included the launch of Motherland Zimbabwe, an international charity based in Birmingham, which had the institutional goals of reversing the brain drain through diaspora skills audits and volunteering schemes. The inaugural family day show was described as 'a celebration of diaspora civic responsibility in the socio-economic development of their motherland Zimbabwe' (Mutize, 2009) and crowds were attracted through the pull of performances by Zimbabwe's renowned musician, Oliver Mtukudzi, alongside Fungisai Zvakavapano and Albert Nyathi.[13]

One of the issues to emerge through these rival groups, conferences and consultations is the problem of how to represent 'the diaspora', and there have been various efforts to set up umbrella groups to facilitate dialogue with governments and others. The 'Coalition of Zimbabwean Groups in the UK', for example, initiated a series of meetings to try to institutionalise an umbrella organisation in late 2009, bringing together not only the new development organisations and church umbrella groups mentioned above, but also longer standing asylum-seeker, human rights and charitable groups, as well as political parties (including MDC[T]-UK, Zapu and MAGGEMM). While this coalition fell apart, other initiatives have been more persistent. The most promising, the Zimbabwe Diaspora Focus Group (ZDFG), headed by Lucia Dube of the Zimbabwe Community Association, was created in response to the FCO's call for Zimbabweans to engage HMG 'with one voice'.[14] The ZDFG brings together representatives of not only the new developmental organisations, but also associations representing human rights, community-based and asylum-seeker support groups, as well as interest groups in culture and the arts, though the topic of how to incorporate political groups is so far unresolved. Such umbrella groups are important given the sheer number and variety of diaspora associations, and their geographical spread across the United Kingdom, which can be bewildering and confusing. Moreover, in relation to some issues there is a clear convergence of opinion across the diaspora's institutional and social cleavages. Such convergence is perhaps particularly evident in relation to demands that responsibilities for development at home are combined with formal political rights.

Diasporic Political Rights at Home: Citizenship, Voting and the Constitution

The diaspora conversations over development at home presume the right to engage from a distance as citizens, and not simply through flows of resources. Yet the rights to participate formally as such will depend on the outcome of the constitution-making process, and the place it accords the diaspora, whether voting rights are extended, and whether dual citizenship will be recognised. The Citizenship of Zimbabwe Amendment Act 2003 prohibits dual citizenship and requires a person with dual citizenship to renounce foreign citizenship to retain their Zimbabwean citizenship. At the same time, only embassy staff and the armed forces have qualified to vote while living beyond Zimbabwe's borders. Thus, the new developmental emphasis in diasporic activism has been combined with a further series of ongoing conversations over political rights.

The growing number of migrant communities who now define themselves as a 'diaspora' can be seen as the outcome of a 'joint project of states and émigrés' (Gamlen, 2008, p. 840). Gamlen argues that although such diaspora populations are often understood as a 'symptom or cure for backwardness', it is increasingly common for states of all sorts to have a 'variety of mechanisms protruding beyond their borders and impacting on various extra-territorial groups' (Gamlen, 2008), while the realities of an increasingly globalised world and new communications technologies have enhanced the possibilities for expatriates to maintain a sense of belonging from beyond national borders (Turner, 1993; Soysal, 1996; Menyhart, 2003). While processes of exclusion in countries of settlement undoubtedly contribute to the desire among migrants to straddle two nations and adopt dual identities (Pedraza, 1999; Yuval-Davis, 1999, p. 126), it is also the case that such diaspora communities often have a difficult relationship with their homeland governments, and adopting citizenship in countries of settlement can be primarily about their quest for security (see Ong, 1998). Thus, at the same time as Zimbabweans abroad have pressed for recognition of citizenship rights at home, they have also taken out citizenship elsewhere in large numbers. In Britain, for example, Zimbabweans are the fifth largest nationality group taking up British citizenship, 5,710 doing so in 2008 alone.[15]

The GoZ has stated that there will be no formal engagement of the diaspora in the constitutional reform exercise that is ongoing in Zimbabwe, owing to lack of financial resources. Yet, diaspora groups interpreted Article 6 of the GPA (that all Zimbabweans should have access to the constitutional consultations) as including Zimbabweans beyond national borders, and have organised meetings and platforms for diaspora members to express and channel their views on constitutional reforms, though it remains unclear how these views can formally be accommodated and combined with those gathered in the homeland. MDC Ministers have welcomed such initiatives—Minister Gorden Moyo, for example, remarked:

> The process of writing a new constitution needs the involvement and contributions from Zimbabweans in the Diaspora. This is based on, not just the sheer numbers of our people living in foreign countries, but also the fact that a Zimbabwean should be considered a citizen of his or her homeland regardless of which country they reside in. (Musoro and Magaisa, 2009, p. 31)

In January 2010, 15 Zimbabwe diaspora groups held a meeting in London to find a strategy for participating in the country's constitution-making process.[16] They formed an umbrella group, the Zimbabwe Constitutional Consultation UK, with Rev. Zeb Manatse as its leader. An outcome of that meeting was a memorandum of understanding aiming to organise 'a Constitutional Review Conference for the Zimbabwean Diaspora in which occasion representatives of the Diaspora shall engage with the leaders and/or representatives of the constitutional reform process in Zimbabwe for the purpose of handing over the results of the consultation representing the views of the Zimbabwean Diaspora' (ZIMCC, 2010). They have also tried to link with diasporic efforts in South Africa, particularly through liaison with the Zimbabwe Exiles Forum.

One controversial proposal is that the diaspora should pay for the privilege of political rights at home. The suggestion of a diaspora tax was mooted in a report commissioned by the World Poverty Institute and launched at the University of Manchester in late 2009, with Zimbabwean Minister of Finance Tendai Biti invited to give an address. The report provided an exploration of the ways in which the diaspora could help the country to move forward: as a source of investment capital, by reversing the brain draw through programmes of skills sharing, temporary and permanent return, and through recognition as citizens (Chimhowu et al., 2009). The authors elaborated the last point as follows:

> Confidence-boosting measures would include allowing dual nationality, restoring voting rights for migrants who hold Zimbabwean citizenship and

creating mechanisms for them to be heard. In exchange, migrants should be prepared to pay an annual tax for retaining Zimbabwean nationality. Clearly this would be controversial but it could be a way for migrants to contribute directly to the state budget. (Chimhowu *et al.*, 2009, p. 126)

The launch attracted widespread discussion, partly because the Zimbabwe diaspora media and other international news agencies attributed the suggested diaspora tax to Tendai Biti, treating it as a policy announcement by the inclusive government. Heated debates flooded the diaspora's media, online websites, forums and internet chat rooms as people questioned how they could be taxed without being allowed to vote. Voices in favour felt such a tax could be introduced only after a number of conditions had been fulfilled, including dual nationality, voting rights, a diaspora MP, and participation in the new constitution (Muponda, 2009); but the majority of contributors to these debates were opposed, and expressed frustration and anger over the proposal, arguing, for example:

Those who fall sick in the Diaspora don't fly back to Gomo Hospital for treatment. Our kids don't commute to Chindunduma High School daily for their education. We don't drink water from Lake Chivero purified and pumped by ZINWA or the Harare City Council. We don't use Zimbabwean roads to drive to work. So why pay tax? (Chamboko, 2009)

Magaisa (2009) argued that such a tax 'has the effect of commodifying citizenship rights for only a section of the country's population'. He continued, 'not only does it undermine the principle of equality for all citizens, it also compartmentalises the right to citizenship, making it potentially inaccessible to those who cannot afford the means to purchase it'. Similarly, Gabriel Shumba, Director of the Pretoria-based Zimbabwe Exiles Forum, remarked: 'Our rights to vote and our rights to citizenship are non-negotiable. This tax suggestion makes the presumption that to be Zimbabwean, you have to pay for those rights and that is unacceptable' (IRIN, 2009).

The lead author of the report, Admos Chimhowu, released a statement to the media denying Minister Tendai Biti had proposed a diaspora tax and blaming the misinformation on 'cut-paste journalism' at the heart of most of Zimbabwean diaspora media (Chimhowu, 2010), and Tendai Biti himself clarified that the proposal was neither his view nor GoZ policy: 'Of course I haven't proposed any such a tax. The report I launched is an independent academic report ... I personally think a citizen tax is not practical. In any event there should never be taxation without representation' (Chimhowu, 2010).

Conclusion

These diasporic conversations over development and citizenship that have taken place since the signing of the GPA are ongoing, and are unlikely to be 'concluded' once and for all. They show how there has been a repositioning within the diaspora and a convergence of interest with homeland and hosting governments around agendas of engagement, replacing the politicised hostilities of the past.

Developmental rhetoric has proved convenient in so far as it appears to paper over conflicts between different interests within the diaspora, homeland and hosting governments, as it provides an apolitical technocratic formulation of a common interest through which to maximise the potential for raising external finance for reconstruction. The new organisations formed in the diaspora focused on development have cast themselves as non-partisan, want to be players in homeland reconstruction and have an elite social base. They have a shared interest in dual citizenship and political rights at home.

Yet these conversations have also revealed tensions and contradictory interests—within the diaspora, between it and the governments involved, as well as within different arms of government and state. While both parties involved in Zimbabwe's unity government have a common interest in encouraging a non-partisan debate over the diaspora's role in development and reconstruction, at the same time the violence that has accompanied constitutional outreach meetings within Zimbabwe has also made it clear that ZANU-PF has every interest in controlling that process and in refusing to extend political rights to diasporans it considers to be MDC supporters.

Regarding the varied interests within the diaspora, the cleavage between those with security in their states of residence and those who are vulnerable to enforced return at some future date has emerged as particularly salient. This cleavage is reflected in divisions between diaspora associations representing different interest groups, and has also shaped relations with the British and Zimbabwean governments, highlighting contradictory interests within each, such as between the FCO and UKBA in Britain. The salience of this diasporic divide is likely to become more pronounced if agendas of reconstruction and development are linked to a large-scale repatriation programme, especially if this occurs in the context of ongoing uncertainty at home and is conceptualised as a final one-way movement rather than as part of an ongoing circulation, in which people may opt to perpetuate attachments to more than one country.

Notes

1. For press coverage, see Dugan (2009) SWRadio Africa (2009), Gonda (2009), Nehanda Radio (2010) and Sibanda (2009). Among those welcoming Tsvangirai were the Zimbabwe Diaspora Development Interface, the Zimbabwe Women's Network, Rebuild Zimbabwe UK Association and the Zimbabwe Association.
2. Home Office, quarterly asylum statistics, available from http://rds.homeoffice.gov.uk/rds/immigration-asylum-stats.html
3. The Home Office published a new operational guidance note in March 2009 to supercede RN, but at the time of writing there has not been a formal appeal to the legal status of the RN case. An appeal is currently scheduled for October 2010.
4. This is clear because the overwhelming majority of claims were not made at 'the border'.
5. In South Africa, there are also new platforms for development, such as the Global Zimbabwe Forum, the Zimbabwe Diaspora Forum, and the Zimbabwe Diaspora Development Chamber. Recently, the diaspora in the United States established the Council for Zimbabwe to achieve humanitarian and development needs.
6. See: http://webarchive.nationalarchives.gov.uk/+/http://www.dfid.gov.uk/Media-Room/News-Stories/2009/Comic-Relief-launches-a-new-20-million-fund/
7. Robert Shooter, DFID representative, address to ZDDI conference, 26 September 2009.
8. http://www.zimdiasporainterface.org
9. Lazarus Muriritirwa, address to ZDDI, 26 September 2009.

10. Emmanuel Munyukwi, CEO Zimbabwe Stock Exchange, address to ZDDI, 26 September 2009.
11. Robert Shooter, DFID representative, ZDDI conference, 26 September 2009.
12. It is beyond the scope of this article to discuss transitional justice activities in the diaspora, led by the ZHRNGO Forum in partnership with the Zimbabwe Association.
13. This is not an exhaustive list.
14. Tamasanqa Zhou, 'Zimbabweans in UK to be consulted on British policy', 27 May 2010. *The Zimbabwean*, 27 May 2010.
15. Figures cited in 'Zimbabweans top list of asylum seekers in UK', NewZimbabwe.com, 23 March 2010.
16. Those involved included the Council of Zimbabwe Christian Leaders, Nottingham Zimbabwe Community Network, Global Zimbabwe Forum, Zimbabwe Investor, Zimbabwe Diaspora Development Interchange, and Zimbabwe Action Group.

References

Bakewell, O. (2008a) Keeping them in their place: the ambivalent relationship between development and migration in Africa, *Third World Quarterly*, 29(7), pp. 1341–1358.

Bakewell, O. (2008b) In search of the diasporas within Africa, *African Diaspora*, 1(1), pp. 5–27.

Black, R. and Gent, S. (2006) Sustainable return in post-conflict contexts, *International Migration*, 44(3), pp. 15–38.

Brinkerhoff, J. (Ed.) (2008) *Diasporas and Development: Exploring the Potential* (Boulder, CO: Lynne Rienner).

Brinkerhoff, J. (2010) The limits of instrumentalizing diasporas: lost opportunities for development, sovereignty and citizenship. Paper presented at the workshop *Agents of Change: The New Governing of Diasporas through Development*, Danish Institute for International Studies, Copenhagen, Denmark.

Chamboko, M. (2009) Diaspora tax: abuse of academic research, *The Zimbabwe Telegraph*, http://www.zimtelegraph.com/?p=5065, accessed 10 June 2010.

Chimhowu, A. (2010) No tax without representation—Biti, *The Zimbabwean*, http://www.thezimbabwean.co.uk/2010010627677/business-news/no-tax-without-representation-biti.html, accessed 10 June 2010.

Chimhowu, A., Bare, T., Chiripanhura, B., Chitekwe-Biti, B., Chung, F., Magure, T., Mambondiyani, L., Manjengwa, J., Matshe, I., Munemo, N., Mtisi, S., NxelE, M. and Sibanda, D. (2009) Moving forward in Zimbabwe—reducing poverty and promoting growth, http://www.bwpi.manchester.ac.uk/research/ResearchAreaProjects/Africa/Moving_forward_in_Zimbabwe_whole_report.pdf, accessed 10 June 2010.

Chindodo, H. (2009) Zimbabwe investment conference set for Coventry, UK, *Zimbabwe Investor Magazine*, http://www.zimbabweinvestor.com/home/?option=com_content&view=article&id=89:zimbabwe-business-investment-conference-oct-2009&catid=1:latest-news&fontstyle=f-smaller, accessed 10 June 2010.

CZCLUK (2009) Zim Christian leaders UK to hold conference, *Nehanda Radio*, Council of Zimbabwean Christian Leaders UK, http://nehandaradio.com/2009/09/17/zim-christian-leaders-uk-to-hold-conference/, accessed 10 June 2010.

Datta, K., McIlwaine, C., Wills, J., Evans, Y., Herbert, J. and May, J. (2007) The new development finance or exploiting migrant labour? Remittance sending among low-paid migrant workers in London, *International Development Planning Review*, 29(1), pp. 43–67.

De Haas, H. (2005) International migration, remittances and development: myths and facts, *Third World Quarterly*, 26(8), pp. 1269–1284.

DFID (1997) *A Challenge for the Twentifirst Century*, White Paper (London: DFID).

DFID (2007) *Making Migration Work for the Poor*, Policy Paper (London: DFID).

Dugan, E. (2009) UK Zimbabweans jeer Tsvangirai as he urges them to return home, *The Independent*, 21 June.

Faist, T. (2008) Migrants as transnational development agents: an inquiry into the newest round of the migration–development nexus, *Population, Space and Place*, 14(1), pp. 21–42.

Gamlen, A. (2008) The emigration state and the modern geo-political imagination, *Political Geography*, 27, pp. 840–856.

Gonda, V. (2009) Zim Vigil deny plotting disruption of Tsvangirai London meeting, SWRadio Africa, http://www.swradioafrica.com/news220609/zimuk220609.htm, accessed 10 June 2010.

Gonda, V. (2010) Has Zuma finally managed to persuade Mugabe to implement GPA? http://www.swradioafrica.com/news190310/zuma190310.htm, accessed 10 June 2010.

GoZ (2010) Draft migration management and diaspora policy of Zimbabwe. Harare, May.

Home Office (2009) Returns to Zimbabwe, Home Office Press Release, 29 October.

IRIN (2009) Expats oppose tax in exchange for voting, http://www.irinnews.org/Report.aspx?ReportId= 87511, accessed 10 June 2010.

Magaisa, A. (2006) Donors, diaspora and Zimbabwe democracy, http://www.kubatana.net/html/archive/, accessed 25 July 2006.

Magaisa, A. (2009) Why 'citizenship tax' is a flawed idea, *The Standard*, www.thestandard.co.zw/.../ 22665-why-citizenship-tax-is-a-flawed-idea.html, accessed 10 June 2010.

McGregor, J. (2009) Associational links with home among Zimbabweans in the UK: reflections on long-distance nationalisms, *Global Networks*, 9(2), pp. 185–208.

McGregor, J. (2010) The making of Zimbabwe's new diaspora, in J. McGregor and R. Primorac (Eds), *Zimbabwe's New Diaspora. Displacement and the Cultural Politics of Survival* (Oxford: Berghahn Books).

Menyhart, R. (2003) Changing identities and changing law: possibilities for a global legal culture, *Indiana Journal of Global Legal Studies*, 10(2), pp. 157–199.

Mercer, C., Page, B. and Evans, M. (2008) *Development and the African Diaspora. Place and the Politics of Home* (London: Zed Press).

Muponda, G. (2009) Zimbabwe diaspora tax wrong idea and misdirected effort, *The Zimbabwe Telegraph*, http://www.zimtelegraph.com/?p=5085, accessed 10 June 2010.

Musoro, L. and Magaisa, A. T. (2009) Engaging the Zimbabwean diaspora on investment, development and migration, http://www.zimdiasporainterface.org/media/invest112009/ZDDI_Conference_Report_Sep2009.pdf, accessed 10 June 2010.

Mutize, N. (2009) Motherland Zimbabwe family show—stage is set, *The Zimbabwean*, http://www.thezimbabwean.co.uk/2009091124430/music/motherland-zimbabwe-family-show-stage-is-set.html, accessed 10 June 2010.

Nehanda Radio (2009) UK diaspora group statement to Tsvangirai, *Nehanda Radio*, http://nehandaradio.com/2009/06/23/uk-diaspora-group-statement-to-tsvangirai/, accessed 10 June 2010.

NZCN (2009) Delegates endorse new body's vision as vital and complimentary to any fasible plan for redevelopment of Zimbabwe, Nottingham Zimbabwe Community Network, http://nzcn.wordpress.com/2009/03/29/zimbabwe-redevelopment-focus-a-practical-paradigm-shift-from-politics-of-sloganeering-and-cardcarrying/, accessed 10 June 2010.

Ong, A. (1998) *Flexible Citizenship: The Cultural Logics of Transnationality* (Durham, NC: Duke University Press).

Orozco, M. (2008) Diasporas and development: issues and impediments, in J. Brinkerhoff (Ed.), *Diasporas and Development: Exploring the Potential* (Boulder, CO: Lynne Rienner), pp. 207–230.

Page, B., Mercer, C. and Evans, M. (2009) Introduction: African transnationalisms and diaspora networks, *Global Networks*, 9(2), pp. 137–140.

Pasura, D. (2008) A fractured diaspora: strategies and identities among Zimbabweans in Britain, PhD Thesis, University of Warwick.

Pasura, D. (2010) Zimbabwean transnational diaspora politics in Britain, in J. McGregor and R. Primorac (Eds), *Zimbabwe's New Diaspora: Displacement and the Cultural Politics of Survival* (London and New York: Berghahn Books).

Pedraza, S. (1999) Assimilation or diasporic citizenship? *Contemporary Sociology*, 28(4), pp. 377–381.

Raftopoulos, B. (2006) Reflections on opposition politics in Zimbabwe: the politics of the Movement for Democratic Change, in B. Raftopoulos and K. Alexander (Eds), *Reflections on Democratic Politics in Zimbabwe* (Cape Town: Institute for Justice and Reconciliation), pp. 6–37.

ROHR (2009) From the Zimbabwe Vigil 'Press Statement from ROHR', SWRadio Africa, 25 June, http://www.swradioafrica.com/pages/ROHR250609.htm, accessed 10 June 2010.

Sibanda, T. (2009) Tsvangirai to address Zimbabweans in London, Saturday, 19 June, http://www.swradioafrica.com/news190609/mttoaddress190609.htm, accessed 10 June 2010.

Soysal, Y. N. (1996) Changing citizenship in Europe: remarks on postnational membership and the national state, in D. Cesarani and M. Fulbrook (Eds), *Citizenship, Nationality and Migration in Europe* (London and New York: Routledge), pp. 19–29.

SWRadio Africa (2009) Zim Vigil deny plotting disruption of Tsvangirai London meeting, SWRadio Africa, 22 June.

Turner, B. (1993) Contemporary problems in the theory of citizenship, in B. Turner (Ed.), *Citizenship and Social Theory* (London: Sage), pp. 1–18.

Woolas, P. (2009) Returns to Zimbabwe. Home Office, http://www.bia.homeoffice.gov.uk/sitecontent/documents/news/wms-returns-to-zimbabwe.pdf, accessed 10 June 2010.

World Bank (2009) African diaspora program, http://go.worldbank.org/O415YQWP90, accessed 10 June 2010.

Yuval-Davis, N. (1999) The multi-layered citizen, *International Feminist Journal of Politics*, 1(1), pp. 119–136.

ZDDI (n.d.) Welcome to our organisation, http://www.zimdiasporainterface.org/index.php?option=com_content&view=article&id=46&Itemid=53, accessed 10 June 2010.

ZGClub (n.d.) About us, http://zgclub.org/about_us.html, accessed 10 June 2010.

ZIMCC (2010) Zimbabwe Constitutional Review Conference, http://www.zimcc.com, accessed 10 June 2010.

The Global Political Agreement as a 'Passive Revolution': Notes on Contemporary Politics in Zimbabwe

BRIAN RAFTOPOULOS

Centre for Humanities Research, University of the Western Cape, and Solidarity Peace Trust, Cape Town, South Africa

ABSTRACT *The Global Political Agreement (GPA) signed between the two Movements for Democratic Change and the Zimbabwe African National Union–Patriotic Front (ZANU-PF) set the change for a new set of political dynamics in Zimbabwe. Although it has not transformed the coercive base of ZANU-PF's support, it has led to new battles for state power and changes in the strategies of the major political parties. The discussion below uses the great Italian Marxist Antonio Gramsci's conception of the 'passive revolution' to understand the changes in the political economy that have marked recent Zimbabwean politics, looking in particular at the different approaches of the three parties to the GPA during this period.*

Introduction

At the heart of the Southern African Development Community (SADC), mediation on the Zimbabwe crisis has been the role of the South African government, which in its position as political and economic leader in Southern Africa has attempted to end the decade-long political crisis in the country. The complexity of this task must be set against the many challenges facing such a process, including the continued recalcitrance of a former liberation movement determined to defy a plebiscite rejecting its continued rule, the impediments in implementing the regional body's protocols on democratic accountability, and the perplexing task of navigating a path between the demands of the 'good governance' agenda of the international community and a still resonant anti-imperialist messaging of a resurgent nationalist politics. In addition to this, then President Mbeki had to deal with strong perceptions of his own bias towards the Mugabe regime throughout the mediation, and a divided opposition in which the different formations used the mediation to deal not only with the Mugabe regime but also with their own contestations over future electoral competition and positioning over possible state power. Thus, as is often the case, such mediation became the site of intense contestation in which national, regional and international forces became embedded in an increasing complexity.

The Mugabe regime through its discourse and destructive party accumulation project represented a provisional, and never total, authoritarian nationalist disengagement away from the dominant international norms on political and economic accountability, and in its defiance confronted a South African mediator whose continental ambitions forced him to negotiate a tightrope between Pan-African sensitivities and the need for Western support for his leadership in a broader African vision (Freeman, 2005). In contrast to this the opposition was constructed through a language of liberal constitutionalism, human rights advocacy and post-nationalist aspirations, with its economic vision, in common with other emergent opposition parties in Africa in the 1990s, never having much option but to conform to the dominant nostrums of neo-liberalism (Olokushi, 1998; Raftopoulos, 2009a). While Mbeki and his successor in the mediation process, Jacob Zuma, maintained an economic prospectus close to that of the Movement for Democratic Change (MDC), the weight of the liberation legacies on the African National Congress (ANC) and the politics of balance in SADC ensured a tight hold on any substantial censure of the Mugabe regime. Faced with this politics of solidarity against the inconsistencies of Western demands on human rights and the application of international justice, the MDC (Tsvangirai) in particular has been hampered as much as helped by the political support of the West. Notwithstanding its clear popular legitimacy at national and international levels, it has had to contend persistently with its image in Southern Africa in the face of its demonisation by the Mugabe regime, and to confront the major obstacles to removing peacefully a former liberation movement from power. In the course of the years since its formation in 1999, the frustrations attendant on dealing with an authoritarian polity have had their own negative effects on unity and accountability in the opposition, resulting in its own pathology of violence and divisions (Raftopoulos, 2006). The major purpose of this discussion is to track the central contours of the SADC mediation and its effects on the politics of the two MDCs, and tangentially the civic movement, in the context of the regional and international pressures that have woven their own agendas into the politics of this period.

A Theoretical Note: The Mediation, the Global Political Agreement and Opposition Politics as a Passive Revolution

One theoretical route to understanding the process underway is to deploy Antonio Gramsci's concept of passive revolution, which in his *Prison Notebooks* functioned as both a concept for historical interpretation and an analytical device for a theoretical problem (Sassoon, 1982, p. 131). Gramsci developed the concept of passive revolution to understand the form of unification that took place in Italy under the Risorgimento. From this analysis he elaborated the passive revolution as a characteristic response of the bourgeoisie to a period of organic crisis and disintegration, in which major transformations in a country's political economy are carried out from above through the agency of the state, without expanding the processes of democratic participation (Simon, 1982). Thus this 'revolution-restoration' that Gramsci viewed as a feature of 'every epoch characterised by complex historical upheavals' (Gramsci, 1978, p. 114) takes place in ways that both transform the relations between the state and civil society and seeks to restructure the model of capital accumulation and the political forms of its existence. The central role of the state, as the constitutive motor for the production and reproduction of the elite, as well its major site of struggle, becomes particularly apparent in the ways that 'hegemony is replaced by statist and bureaucratic domination' (Buci-Glucksman, 1979, p. 22), or what Gramsci referred to as 'dictatorship without hegemony'. Furthermore as Buci-Glucksman (1979) noted, one should not assume that the theory results in a dualism between production and politics; on the contrary, the politics of the passive revolution need to be located in the changed production relations of a particular period, in which, 'through the legislative interventions of the state far-reaching modifications are being introduced into the country's economic structure' (Gramsci, 1982, p. 120). Moreover, the structural changes in the economy as a result of state intervention and coercion undermine the capacity of popular forces to develop their own autonomous politics and to organise alternative hegemonic alliances.

An analysis of Zimbabwean politics over the last decade can certainly be read through the conceptual lens of a passive revolution, in which major changes on the land, though unleashed through the agency of war veterans, remained largely under the control of the state, in a process of land distribution that has, for the most part, been carried out through a violent and coercive process that has largely politically marginalised the majority of the population. Similarly, the broader struggles for indigenisation of the economy, and in particular the looting of the large diamond deposits in the Chiadzwa area, have added another dimension to the militarisation of the state, the terror of the population and the crude accumulation of the elite. These policy interventions, in addition to the broader deleterious economic policies of the Mugabe state, have transformed relations not only between the state and civil society but also between the state and existing capital. However, the challenges such changes have presented for the regime, in terms of both national legitimacy and punitive international responses, forced the Zimbabwe African National Union–Patriotic Front (ZANU-PF) into a temporary power-sharing deal that it did not want, but was forced to accept. Thus, in important ways the Global Political Agreement (GPA) brokered through SADC could be seen as one major aspect of the passive revolution that has taken place in Zimbabwe, in which a ruling party facing an organic political and economic crisis has used the space to reconfigure and renegotiate the terms of its existence with the opposition, civil society and the international community. It continues to face challenges to the national legitimacy and international re-engagement it seeks, particularly with the continued 'sanctions' against the regime. However, because of the growing entrenchment of the military-economic elite in Zimbabwe's political economy and the shield of regional political solidarity along with, for the moment, the Chinese and Russian protection at the United Nations, under which they brave their politics, the crisis in Zimbabwe is likely to be a lengthy process. Added to this, the political legacies and grotesque economic accumulation of Mugabe's party are not likely to disappear even if there were to be a change of ruling party in the near future.

In another application of the concept of passive revolution, it may also be argued that the politics of the MDC and the civic movement under the GPA can best be understood under the register of this analytical tool, for several reasons. Both formations of the MDC have also been pushed into the GPA as a result of a combination of: state repression and violence against the structures of the MDC; the inability of the opposition to translate their electoral victory in 2008 into state power in the face of ZANU-PF's control of the coercive arms of the state; the structural erosion and political exhaustion of its support base, particularly in urban areas, as well as the weakening of the civic movement as a result of similar factors; and the limits of Western diplomacy in removing the Zimbabwe question from the SADC regional bloc in which Mugabe's Pan-Africanist message and the shortcomings of the regional body itself have ensured Mugabe regional cover against the thunderous imprecations of the West (Solidarity Peace Trust, 2008, 2009, 2010).

Drawing on the theoretical position above, it is clear that the changes in the structures and relations of production as a result of the changes in the accumulation model and forms of employment in the country, particularly the rapid informalisation of labour, have had a number of effects. They have severely eroded the structural basis for labour and opposition mobilisation in a more informally constituted economy, in which the discipline and modalities of formal organisation built up by a once formidable labour movement have been lost to the different rhythms of survivalist opportunism endemic in the more precarious conditions of informal livelihoods. In the words of Hammar *et al.* (2010), the crisis of displacement that has characterised the historic upheavals in the Zimbabwean economy has reshaped patterns of production, accumulation and exchange, reconfigured state power, and led to conflicting claims and obligations. One might add that the *kukiya-kiya* (wheeler/dealer, getting by) survival strategies that have come to constitute a dominant form of social relations in the informalised urban area (Jones, 2010) have emerged as a result of the suppression of the more disciplined and public forms of organisation associated with the labour movement. With the removal of this more accountable form of organisation from the public sphere, such popular organisations and their allies have seen their past attempts to build an alternative hegemonic project severely undermined, a major result of ZANU-PF's party accumulation and authoritarian restructuring from above (Raftopoulos, 2009b).

The discourse of human rights so effectively deployed by the civic movement since the 1990s has also had an ambiguous effect on the politics of democratic struggle in Zimbabwe. On the one hand the language of civic and constitutional rights has greatly expanded the debate on democratic participation in the context of a long tradition of such rights struggles around, for example, the rule of law, the vote, urban and rural governance, women's rights, workers' rights in the anti-colonial struggles, as well as the strategic use of universalist claims around citizenship to confront the repressive constructions of the settler state (Ranger and Bhebe, 2001; Ranger, 2003). Moreover, the politics of the human rights movement has created a strong tradition of research, reporting and advocacy on rights issues at national, regional and international levels that has made Zimbabwe one of the most documented countries in this area on the continent. The vigilance and courage of civic activists in the country have made them the scourge of the Mugabe regime, providing a series of damning reports and advocacy interventions that have helped to undermine the legitimacy of the regime.

The discourse of human rights, however, has also been constructed in a global context in which, since the 1990s, aid from the EU and the OECD has linked neo-liberal economic policies to the 'good governance' agenda and political condition-ality, in which the emphasis has been placed on elections and formal political and civic rights, rather than on social and economic rights (Abrahamson, 1997). Under this framework, it is believed that elections will 'broaden and deepen political participation', and serve 'not just as a foundation stone but a key generator of further democratic reforms' (Carothers, 2002, p. 8). Through US state-funded organisations such as the National Democratic Institute, the International Repub-lican Institute and Freedom House, this dominant political perspective of democracy assistance is funnelled, in which aid is targeted at key political institutions such as political parties and civic groups, 'with the hope of catalytic effects' (Carothers, 2009, p. 5). Much of the human rights discourse and lobbying in Zimbabwe is constructed through this framework, with little analysis of political economy issues, the broader effects of global neo-liberalism on local debates, or the politics of regional dynamics in SADC.[1] Moreover, notwithstanding the recurrent problems of violence and accountability in the MDCs, there has been too little critical attention given to this matter in the civic movement because of the strategic priority of removing the Mugabe regime. The result is that there is likely to be little preparedness for the problems that have confronted other pro-democracy movements coming to power, namely weakly institutionalised political systems, and the challenges of succession and executive dominance that drive such parties (Rakner, 2010).

The making of such a critique is not aimed at undermining both the strategic and political importance of the human rights debate in Zimbabwe, for as has been pointed out above this has a long historical record behind it. Nor do such criticisms vitiate the need for legitimate elections. However, such interventions are meant to contextualise the current import of the human rights debate, and to take note of its limitations and disabling elements in the interpellation of people as juridical rather than more broadly political subjects, and as part of the language of the new form of imperialism (Neocosmos, 2006, p. 374). This linkage becomes particularly perilous when the national social base and local forms of civil society from which to launch such universalist claims have been severely eroded by structural economic crisis and political repression, and the major advocacy pressure is emanating from external sources. Drawing once again from Gramsci, it can be noted that when such pressures are not tightly linked to a strong national social base, there is a greater likelihood of them becoming extensions of international developments, and passive citizens in a project beyond their control (Gramsci, 1982, pp. 116–170). In such circumstances emphasis for political change is placed on changes in the control of the state, with little thought given to the broader developmental issues required for substantive transformation.

Tracking the SADC Mediation

Having set out this general theoretical argument, this section will turn to the detail of the SADC mediation. As the Zimbabwe crisis unfolded from the late 1990s around the questions of post-colonial democratisation and the legacies of colonial inequality, the politics of the crisis posed serious dilemmas not only for Zimbabweans, but also for the region and South Africa in particular. On becoming President of South Africa in 1999, Thabo Mbeki, faced with the politics of solidarity and sovereignty in SADC and the African Union, was determined to avoid the pitfalls of unilateralism that the South African state encountered in its dealings with Nigeria, Lesotho and the Democratic Republic of Congo (DRC) in the 1990s. The post-9/11 world and regime change strategy that became a hallmark of US foreign policy under George W. Bush also heightened the sensitivities of African states to opposition movements on the continent viewed as the agents of such a strategy.

The Mbeki government was also very sensitive about being seen as the regional bully, pushing its own agendas in conflict situations, and hence continuing the ambitions of the apartheid state. Thus, on the Zimbabwe question South Africa's broader ambition of leading the continent and becoming a global player meant that it had 'to walk the tightrope of keeping South Africa's continental ambitions alive (by not coming out in opposition to Mugabe's regime) without totally sacrificing Western support' (Freeman, 2005, p. 156), seeking also to link the 'rhetoric and energy' of Pan-Africanism to a struggle to reform the global order (Habib, 2009). In a paper written on Zimbabwe soon after taking over as head of state, Mbeki stated a key aspect of his assessment of the problem and his attitude to the 'party of revolution', ZANU-PF:

> Of critical importance ... is the obvious necessity to ensure that Zimbabwe does not end up in a situation of isolation, confronted by an array of international forces it cannot defeat, condemned to sink into an ever-deepening social and economic crisis that would result in the reversal of so many of the gains of the national democratic revolution. It is also important that the party of revolution should consider its internationalist responsibilities to the rest of the Continent and especially to southern Africa, given the reality that events in any one of our countries has an impact on other countries particularly in our region. (Mbeki, 2008, pp. 66–67)

In breaking down the policy of 'quiet diplomacy' that led from Mbeki's assessment of the Zimbabwe crisis, Jeremy Cronin (2004), a key member of the Alliance in South Africa, noted three phases in the strategic approach of the South African government to Zimbabwe by 2004. In the first phase between the formation of the MDC and the 2000 general election in Zimbabwe, the MDC was viewed as 'both a symptom of weaknesses and errors committed by ZANU-PF, and as a challenge that could (and should) be warded off'. To deal with the challenge the South African government encouraged a combination of sustainable and stabilising macroeconomic policies, pushed by the 'reformers' in ZANU-PF, combined with a modernised electoral strategy that would avoid violence. This, it was hoped, would avoid the danger of a 'regime change' via the ballot box. This strategy was soon confronted by the resistance of key ZANU-PF factions to any reform strategy, as well as the party's preference for violent, patronage-based mobilisation geared towards maintaining ethnic balance in ZANU-PF. It also failed to account for the rapid accumulation strategies that the economic crisis presented for the ruling party leadership.

In the second phase during the run up to the 2002 Presidential election, after the surprising success of the MDC in the 2000 general election, the support and social base of the MDC could not be so easily dismissed. However, the Mbeki government had three concerns around the MDC. First was the fear that the Zimbabwean military and security sectors would not accept an elected MDC government, and a statement to that effect on the eve of the 2002 election merely confirmed that fear. Second, the South African government was concerned that the MDC would not have the capacity to run a state, and that this weakness would very quickly lead to a weak, unstable state on its border. Third, the concern that the MDC was too close to the West increased anxieties about its future role in the region.[2] Given this assessment, Cronin described the hopes of the South African government in the following terms:

> Regime change is one thing, the practical consequences in the immediate aftermath (as the present reality in Iraq reminds us) is quite another. For these reasons our government hoped that, as a best case scenario, ZANU-PF would win a free and fair election. If, however, elections were less than free and fair, but the ZANU-PF candidate was still declared the winner, the fall-back scenario would be a pragmatic recognition of a Mugabe 'victory', but in return for this recognition, ZANU-PF would be expected to move immediately to establishing a GNU with the opposition. (Cronin, 2004, p. 5; see also Landsberg, 2004)

The highly contested nature of the 2002 election, resulting in a further polarisation of Zimbabwean politics and the West–Africa divide on the Zimbabwe crisis, scuttled this scenario.

In the aftermath of another highly contested general election in 2005 and the deepening divide around Zimbabwe that ensued, the Mbeki government continued to place its emphasis on the need for a national dialogue between the major parties, leading to a free and fair election. It was also hoped that this eventuality would result in the removal of the sanctions, and that the heightened succession battle in ZANU-PF would lead to a Mugabe exit and a reformed ZANU-PF agenda, on the understanding that such a transition would have the support of the military.

This analysis of the Mbeki government is interesting because, in the view of this writer, its central theses provided that paradigm for the mediation attempts that followed. Moreover, this was an assessment that largely framed the constraints of the Zuma administration that succeeded Mbeki. The unified MDC up to 2005 shared Mbeki's objective to move towards a free and fair election, but clearly differed with him on the future role of ZANU-PF. In the early attempt by President Obasanjo of Nigeria and President Mbeki of South Africa to mediate a settlement in 2002, the MDC stated this position clearly:

> ... we in the MDC stand ready to embark on a process of national reconciliation and national healing. But such a process must be anchored in a sound foundation characterised by an unconditional return to legitimacy. This can only be achieved through fresh presidential elections, under free and fair

conditions and supervised and monitored by the region, the continent and the international community. (Tsvangirai, 2002, p. 3)

For its part, ZANU-PF noted that its central position was tied to legitimacy, not derived primarily from an electoral process, but from the sovereignty achieved as a result of the liberation struggle:

> The huge sacrifices which accompanied our rise to statehood makes the sovereignty of this country sacred and sacrosanct, a non-negotiable issue we are duty bound to uphold, defend and augment for all times as Zimbabweans. No one party around or to come, can ever arrogate to itself the right to negotiate our sovereignty. Indeed, no one party can ask for permission to diminish our sovereignty through associations, whether national or international, which may threaten it. (Chinamasa, 2002, pp. 5–6)

These competing discourses continued to run right through the positions of ZANU-PF and the two MDCs in the period leading to and in the wording of the GPA signed in September 2008, with the language of much of the civic movement according closely with that of the MDCs. Moreover, in Mbeki's early treatise on the Zimbabwe situation, mentioned above, one could detect both discourses, with a definite partiality towards the language of the liberation movement in Zimbabwe (Moore, 2010).

After the Extra-ordinary Summit of the Heads of State and Government of SADC in Dar-es-Salaam on 29 March 2007 mandated President Mbeki to act as facilitator between ZANU-PF and the two MDCs, Mbeki stated that the dialogue should achieve the following:

- Endorse the decision to hold parliamentary and presidential elections in 2008.
- Agree on the steps that must be taken … to ensure that everybody concerned accepts the results of the elections as being truly representative of the will of the people.
- Agree on the measures that all political parties and other social forces must implement and respect to create the necessary climate that will facilitate such acceptance.

Mbeki also put forward his hope that the projected 2008 election would 'provide a golden and strategic opportunity' to 'begin the process leading to the normalisation of the situation in Zimbabwe' and the 'resumption of its development and reconstruction process intended to achieve a better life for all Zimbabweans, on a sustained basis'.[3] In response the two MDCs set out their conditions for a free and fair election, stressing that the existing constitution was the 'root cause of many of the problems' that beset the country, and that therefore new elections 'should only take place after a new democratic national Constitution comes into operation' (MDC, 2007). Predictably, ZANU-PF responded that the Land Question, 'and not the so called need for a new Constitution, alleged human rights violations or alleged lack of the rule of law or a declining economy' was at the centre of the Zimbabwe situation (ZANU-PF, 2007).

With electoral conditions and constitutional reform at the heart of the mediation process, Mbeki attempted to cajole both sides into an election as soon as possible, going so far as to make exaggerated claims in his report to the SADC organ on politics, defence and security, in February 2008, that the parties had reached agreement on all substantive issues relating to the political situation, noting that 'the only outstanding matter relates to the procedure to be followed in enacting the agreed draft constitution' (SADC, 2008). A joint statement by both MDCs protested against Mbeki's report and the subsequent SADC statement, pointing out that the issues of the date of the elections, the time-frame for the implementation of the agreed reforms and the 'process and manner of the making and enactment of a new constitution were not matters of procedure but of substance and went to the heart of the matter'. Moreover, Mugabe's unilateral announcement of the election date 'amounted to a repudiation of the SADC dialogue by ZANU-PF' (MDC, 2008).

After the electoral victories of the MDC-T in particular in the general and first round presidential elections of 2008, and the ensuing illegitimate presidential run-off in June of that year, the resumed SADC mediation resulted in the September 2008 GPA. ZANU-PF has used its continued monopoly over the state's coercive forces to limit the implementation of those aspects of the GPA that could potentially open up democratic spaces in the Zimbabwean polity. In particular, Mugabe's party has refused to consider any security sector reform, for fear of unravelling the centre of the party. Moreover, although there has been some movement in the establishment of new electoral and human rights commissions, the opening up of the media space has been confined to the print media, with the more popular electronic media still firmly under party control. In the area of constitutional reform, the agreement under Section 6.1 of the GPA to carry out the process under the auspices of a Select Committee of Parliament represented a position in which the MDC compromised on the process in order to try to gain as much as possible from the content. It is likely therefore that the substantive content of the new constitution will be composed of the compromised Kariba Draft signed by the negotiators in September 2007.

It bears repeating that the lack of internal leverage by both MDCs against Mugabe's authoritarian project, notwithstanding the electoral majority of the MDC-T, gave them little room but to negotiate the compromises of the GPA. Since entering the Inclusive Government in February 2009, the MDCs have on the one hand pushed for full implementation of the GPA, while on the other hand they have struggled to position themselves in a state whose structure is still largely shaped by the imperatives of ZANU-PF's military-economic elite. The seemingly endless struggle over the outstanding issues overlaps with both these processes and has once again cast the MDCs not only against ZANU-PF but also against each other, and in a few cases led to agreement between MDC-M and ZANU-PF over the interpretation of the outstanding issues.[4] With their politics henceforth focused largely on working within the state, the effects of this emphasis on the MDCs have been twofold. At one level the already difficult relationship that existed between the two MDC formations during the mediation process grew more antagonistic both in the run up to the 2008 elections and in the period of further mediation that followed. After a brief attempt to draw up principles of cooperation in April 2007, lack of agreement over parliamentary selection and the jostling for future positions in the state ensured a growing animosity between the two formations with the dominant

MDC-T, seeing little gain in developing a parliamentary pact with a rump of the original party, whose prospects beyond another election looked terminal. The relationship between the two formations continued to be difficult in the Inclusive Government, with the MDC-T and much of the civic movement viewing the Mutambara formation as a temporary irritant, undeserving of its place in such an agreement. That such intolerance should persist in the ranks of the opposition remains a disturbing feature of Zimbabwe's political culture.

At another level the focus on state power, away from party organisational work, led to increasing tensions within each party. In the MDC-T, organisational and structural problems in the party as well as internal party violence, which led to the split in 2005 (Raftopoulos, 2006), recurred in 2010 because the issues were left largely unattended to. Reported struggles in this party have, as in 2005, focused on the tensions between the offices of the President and that of the Secretary General, with the role of the 'kitchen cabinet' once again coming to the fore (*Zimbabwe Independent*, 2010). Apart from the changed contexts in which these tensions emerged, there are three differences between the struggles in 2010 and those preceding the 2005 tragedy. First, in the earlier period the donors largely supported the removal of Welshman Ncube, the Secretary General of the united MDC and one of the leading protagonists in the 2005 split, as they saw him as an obstacle in strengthening the powers of the Presidency. In the recent period the donors were very much behind Tendai Biti because of his management of the economy (*Zimbabwe Independent*, 2010). Second, in 2005 Ncube's social base in the party was weak and the ethnicisation of the politics of the split led to a rapid demonisation of his person, not only in the party but also in the allied civic movement. In the current period, although Tsvangirai's position in the party and the country is unassailable, Biti's position is much stronger that Ncube's was in 2005. In a further twist to this internal struggle, Mugabe was reported to have warned Tsvangirai against removing Biti both because of his effectiveness as a minister (*Zimbabwe Independent*, 2010) and arguably because of Biti's role in negotiating a future normalisation of relations between Zimbabwe and the International Financial Institutions (IFI). Third, it is highly unlikely that the current tensions in the party will lead to a split, as they did in 2005. This is because Biti has neither a sufficient political base nor the political space in the current conjuncture for such a move, and Tsvangirai, on his part, feels the divisions can be dealt with within the party structures without threatening his position. Both are aware that another split in the MDC would be disastrous.

In the smaller Mutambara MDC, the bleak prospects of surviving an election in the near future, as well as the severely weakened state of the party, have led to several defections, criticisms of the party leadership, and the formation of yet another splinter group, MDC 99, led by a former member of this formation and a student leader in the 1990s, Job Sikhala. With little prospect of surviving outside the current arrangements of the state, it is not surprising that such squabbles emerged over existing positions (*NewsDay*, 2010; *Financial Gazette*, 2010).

All these developments signified internal party tensions in the context of a broader political parabola still shaped by the destructive politics of ZANU-PF, in which the electoral power of Tsvangirai's party had yet to provide the leverage to shift the military power at the heart of Mugabe's party. In the face of these challenges, the role of the international community proved equally problematic. Since the early

2000s, sanctions imposed against key figures in the Mugabe regime by the United States and the EU, combined with the lack of new development assistance from the IFIs, have been the major strategic weapon used by the West in attempts to push the regime into political and economic liberalisation. The language of the sanctions has been cast as punishment against the regime for its use of political violence and intimidation, lack of free and fair elections, human rights abuses, erosion of the rule of law, a land acquisition process that undermined the protection of property, and the abuses of the media and judiciary (MacDermott, 2009).

After the signing of the GPA, however, the politics of the sanctions issue became a further site of the ambiguity in the Inclusive Government, and thus a source of renewed rhetorical fire from Mugabe's nationalist turrets. The GPA committed the parties to work 'together in re-engaging the international community with a view to bringing to an end the country's international isolation' (Global Political Agreement, 2008, p. 4). In the 'Final Report of the Negotiators on the Post-Maputo Interparty Dialogue', issued in April 2010, it was also agreed that the principals 'should meet and consider the issuance of a statement and the convening of a press conference restating commitment to the GPA, and the removal of sanctions ... and the implementation and execution of a consistent message on the question of sanctions'. SADC persistently supported such a position, and Mbeki's successor Jacob Zuma repeated it during his state visit to the United Kingdom in March 2010.

Both the EU and the United States on their part argued that the removal of sanctions could only be linked to a full implementation of the GPA, and that until such time the measures would remain in place with assistance restricted to the humanitarian sphere. The US and British governments in particular were always clear that any full re-engagement between Zimbabwe and the international community depended on the removal of Mugabe. At the end of 2008, a few months after the signing of the GPA, the US Assistant Secretary of State for Africa, Jendayi Fraser, was categorical about this: 'Mugabe is a barrier to progress, and is not likely to be a viable partner towards the successful implementation of the September deal' (*Business Day*, 2008). This position was stated more diplomatically by the Foreign Secretary of the new British government in June 2010:

> This government will focus on supporting a process that gives Zimbabweans a chance to state their democratic preferences, and that leads to a stable government genuinely representing the people's will. It is vital that elections, when held, must be concluded in a manner that allows Zimbabweans to express their opinions in an informed and free way and without fear of violence and intimidation. We will be working with the international and regional community to ensure that this can happen. (Zimbabwe Vigil, 2010)

The debate on Zimbabwe's future thus took on, once again, the complexion of an Africa versus the West confrontation, with Mugabe, and SADC, arguing that the EU and the United States should respect the terms of an African-negotiated solution. With the human rights groups generally supportive of the position of the donors, advocacy around the sanctions issue appeared as an issue largely driven by outside actors, with the local advocacy groups in a junior, supportive role. The advocacy around the suspension of Zimbabwe in the Kimberley Process over the human rights abuses related to the mining of diamonds in the Chiadzwa area appeared in a similar light, notwithstanding the arrest of local civic activist Farai Maguwu. The key point that emerged from these forms of pressure was that with a severely weakened local civic base and in the context of an opposition that had signed up to a regionally negotiated power pact, these measures took on the appearance of a politics driven largely by external sources, thus subordinating local forces to a different kind of passive revolution. In July 2010 the negotiators of the three parties in the GPA held talks with the Vice-President of the EU and the Commissioner for Development Andris Piebalgs, under Article 96 of the Cotonou Agreement, with the aim of moving the dialogue between the parties forward, with the discussion particularly focused on constitutional and security reforms. After the talks Ashton stated that the EU 'appreciates some progress made implementing the Global Political Agreement in Zimbabwe and remains ready to continue the dialogue and to respond flexibly and positively to any clear signals of further concrete progress'. Moreover, following this meeting the mandated parties in Harare were tasked with defining the indicators, setting the timetable for the achievement of concrete objectives based on their respective roadmaps of commitments, and monitoring progress (Europa, 2010). It remains to be seen whether this will be a step towards the 'normalisation of the situation' in Zimbabwe envisaged by Mbeki.

Conclusion

This paper has attempted to argue, using the Gramscian concept of 'passive revolution', that Zimbabwe's democratic forces have become part of a passive revolution through two processes. In one part of this configuration, notwithstanding the electoral popularity of Tsvangirai's MDC, the repressive anchor of the Mugabe regime, itself pushed into a negotiated settlement by a variety of factors, has largely shaped the contours of this settlement, forcing the opposition to adjust to ZANU-PF's reconfiguration of the state and its relations to capital from above. Moreover, ZANU-PF has carried out this manoeuvre under the cover of the regional body, itself constrained by its own limitations. In another part of this conjuncture, the control of an important tool of leverage for change in the country's political relations by external forces has placed the opposition and civic forces in a subordinate role to broader global agendas on political and economic change. In this context, the politics of the opposition and civil society groupings could be understood as being in a defensive mode, fighting to institutionalise forms of politics that could establish a broader basis for imagining and carrying out alternative political visions. Moreover, the MDC-T in particular has had to adapt its political positioning to the imperatives of the GPA, the politics of SADC, and the demands of its supporters in the West. In this field of force the persistent calls for new legitimate elections have been understandable, but clearly face enormous odds. Finding a way through the problem remains a complex challenge that involves not just an electoral strategy but a broader development vision.

Notes

1. A good example of this trajectory of research and advocacy is the Research and Advocacy Unit, What are the Options for Zimbabwe? Dealing with the Obvious!, Harare, 4 May 2010, where the lack of an historical sensibility is palpable.

2. I heard these concerns on many occasions between 2002 and 2007 in my discussions with key figures in the Mbeki administration and the leadership of the two MDCs.
3. Letter from Thabo Mbeki to Morgan Tsvangirai and Arthur Mutambara, cc President Robert Mugabe, 4 April 2007.
4. See the Final Report of the Negotiators on the Post Maputo Interparty Dialogue, April 2010. The MDC-M refers to the smaller formation of the MDC, led by former student leader and prominent academic Prof. Arthur Mutambara, which emerged after the split in the organisation in 2005.

References

Abrahamson, R. (1997) The victory of popular forces or passive revolution? A neo-Gramscian perspective on democratisation, *Journal of Modern African Studies*, 35(1), pp. 129–152.

Buci-Glucksman, C. (1979) State, transition and passive revolution, in C. Mouffe (Ed.), *Gramsci and Marxist Theory* (London: Routledge and Kegan Paul).

Business Day (2008) US insists Mugabe has to be evicted, 22 December.

Carothers, T. (2002) The end of the transition paradigm, *Journal of Democracy*, 13(1), pp. 5–21.

Carothers, T. (2009) Democracy assistance: political vs. developmental, *Journal of Democracy*, 20(1), pp. 5–19.

Chinamasa, P. (2002) Opening remarks by Patrick Chinamasa, head of the ZANU-PF team to the ZANU-PF-MDC dialogue, Parliament Building, Harare, 8 April.

Cronin, J. (2004) Towards a clearer strategic analysis of the Zimbabwean crisis, unpublished mimeo.

Final report of the negotiators on the post-Maputo interparty dialogue (2010) Harare.

Financial Gazette (2010) Daggers drawn for Mutambara, 15–21 April, pp. 1, 27.

Freeman, L. (2005) South Africa's Zimbabwe policy: unravelling the contradictions, *Journal of Contemporary African Studies*, 23(2), pp. 147–172.

Global Political Agreement (2008) Agreement between the Zimbabwe African National Union–Patriotic Front (Zanu-PF) and the two Movement for Democratic Change (MDC) Formations, on resolving the challenges facing Zimbabwe. Harare.

Gramsci, A. (1978) *Selections from Prison Notebooks* (London: Lawrence and Wishart).

Habib, A. (2009) South Africa's foreign policy: hegemonic aspirations, neoliberal orientations, and global transformations, *South African Journal of International Affairs*, 16(2), pp. 143–159.

Hammar, A., McGregor, J. and Landau, L. (2010) Introduction: displacing Zimbabwe: crisis and construction in Southern Africa, *Journal of Southern African Studies*, 36(2), pp. 263–283.

Jones, J. (2010) Nothing is straight in Zimbabwe: the rise of the kukiya-kiya economy, 2000–2008, *Journal of Southern African Studies*, 36(2), pp. 285–299.

Lansberg, C. (2004) *The Quiet Diplomacy of Liberation: International Politics and South Africa's Transition* (Johannesburg: Jacana Press).

MacDermott, J. (2009) *Breaking the Mould in Zimbabwe: Pragmatic Engagement at a Critical Juncture* (Stockholm: FOI, Swedish Defence and Research Agency).

Mbeki, T. (2008) The Mbeki–Mugabe papers: what Mbeki told Mugabe, *New Agenda*, 30, pp. 56–72.

MDC (2007) MDC submission to the South African President Thabo Mbeki: SADC appointed mediator on Zimbabwe.

MDC (2008) MDC press statement on the failed SADC dialogue on the crisis in Zimbabwe.

Media Release from the Zimbabwe Vigil (2010) www.zimvigil.co.uk/ZimVigil-Diary-Entries/zimbabwe-vigil-diary-29th-May-2010.html, accessed 8 November 2010.

Moore, D. (2010) A decade of disquieting diplomacy: South Africa, Zimbabwe and the ideology of national democratic revolution, 1999–2009, *History Compass*, 8(8), pp. 752–767.

Neocosmos, M. (2006) Can a human rights culture enable emancipation? Clearing the theoretical ground for a renewal of critical sociology, *South African Review of Sociology*, 37(2), pp. 356–380.

NewsDay (2010) Defections hit Mutambara's MDC, 26 June.

Olokushi, A.O. (1998) *The Politics of Opposition in Contemporary Africa* (Uppsala: Nordic Africa Institute).

Raftopoulos, B. (2006) Reflections on opposition politics in Zimbabwe: the politics of the Movement for Democratic Change (MDC), in B. Raftopoulos and K. Alexander (Eds), *Reflections on Democratic Politics in Zimbabwe* (Cape Town: Institute for Justice and Reconciliation).

Raftopoulos, B. (2009a) The MDC, neoliberalism and the challenges of post-colonial change in Zimbabwe, *Openspace*, 3(1), pp. 62–65.

Raftopoulos, B. (2009b) The crisis in Zimbabwe 1998–2008, in B. Raftopoulos and A. Mlambo (Eds), *Becoming Zimbabwe: A History from the Pre-colonial Period to 2008* (Harare/Johannesburg: Weaver/Jacana Press).

Rakner, L. (2010) The paradox of party institutionalisation in a liberal era. The cases of Zambia and Malawi. Paper presented at a *Workshop on Election Processes, Liberation Movements and Democratic Change in Africa*, Maputo, 8–11 April.

Ranger, T. (2003) *The Historical Dimensions of Democracy and Human Rights in Zimbabwe, Volume 2: Nationalism, Democracy and Human Rights* (Harare: University of Zimbabwe Publications).

Ranger, T. and Bhebe, N. (2001) *The Historical Dimensions of Democracy and Human Rights in Zimbabwe, Volume 1: Pre-colonial and Colonial Legacies* (Harare: University of Zimbabwe Publications).

Sassoon, A. (1982) Passive revolution and the politics of reform, in A. S. Sassoon (Ed.), *Approaches to Gramsci* (London: Writers and Readers).

Simon, R. (1982) *Gramsci's Political Thought* (London: Lawrence and Wishart).

Solidarity Peace Trust (2008) *Punishing Dissent, Silencing Citizens: The Zimbabwe Elections 2008* (Johannesburg: Solidarity Peace Trust).

Solidarity Peace Trust (2009) *Walking a Thin Line: The Political and Humanitarian Challenges Facing Zimbabwe's GPA Leadership—and its Ordinary Citizens* (Johannesburg: Solidarity Peace Trust).

Solidarity Peace Trust (2010) *What Options for Zimbabwe?* (Johannesburg: Solidarity Peace Trust).

South African Development Community (SADC) (2008) Media statement on the extraordinary meeting of the Southern African Development Community (SADC) organ on politics, defence and security, Addis Abada, Ethiopia, 4 February.

South African Liason Office (2009) *A Country Focus Paper on South Africa's Relations with Zimbabwe: The Politics and Power of Policy* (Cape Town: SALO).

Tsavangirai, M. (2002) A Brief for President Olusegun Obasanjo, Republic of Nigeria and President Thabo Mbeki, Republic of South Africa. Harare.

ZANU-PF (2007) SADC initiated dialogue: Government of Zimbabwe/ZANU-PF position paper.

Zimbabwe Independent (2010) How Biti escaped cabinet dismissal, 25 June–1 July.

Postscript: Making Do in Hybrid House

Ranka Primorac and Stephen Chan

The building had been crudely extended. A wall had been knocked down to the left and concrete blocks hastily laid to add another seven metres. Such architectural genius has left us with a hybrid building, the likes of which you could only find if you looked hard. The right of the building was constructed of proper burnt bricks, professionally built in every respect. You could see the dividing line where the cheap concrete blocks had been used. Aesthetics aside, we were all grateful for the accommodation though it rattled a little during heavy storms.

(Huchu 2010: 2)

This description of a building, from the beginning of Tendai Huchu's fast-paced first novel, *The Hairdresser of Harare*, is an apt metaphor of both the political arrangement scrutinised in this book and its cultural resonances. Zimbabwe was once, memorably, imagined in fiction as 'the house of hunger' (Marechera 1978). The author of the metaphor– the late, great Zimbabwean writer Dambudzo Marechera–has since gained trans-national literary fame for rejecting binary thinking in all of its forms: critics have remarked in particular on his lampooning of both colonial and postcolonial nationalisms (Veit-Wild and Chennels 1999), and on his repeated transgressions of boundaries related to gender and sexuality (Shaw 2005).

The cover of the 1993 African Writers Series edition of *The House of Hunger* bears a picture of man (his blackness rendered in blue, against predominantly blue-and-yellow background) with strange things literally coming out of his head. Younger Zimbabwean writers have registered a post-modernist bemusement with the existential angst emanating from Marechera's life and work (Chikwava 2010). His opus straddles the historical transition from colonialism to independence, when adopting a critical attitude towards the nation and its leaders (many of whom are still in power today) was no laughing matter.

By contrast, the cover of Huchu's novel–published since the power sharing deal—is deliberately styled to suggest 'popular' or even 'chick lit': against a uniform blue-green background, a cartoon-style silhouette of a girl's profile is outlined, with further, filigree detail added at the edges of the outline: the border of the girl's afro is also a city skyline (which includes embracing heterosexual lovers), with a pink comb protruding from the hair morphing into a broken heart. You cannot buy Huchu's book in Harare's famous Book Café, because it no longer functions as a bookshop (see Primorac), but you can

.y it at Johannesburg's Oliver Tambo International Airport, alongside other regional
terary offerings of the moment. Whereas Marechera's tragedy-tinged anarchism called
for a serious critical and philosophical engagement, Huchu (the first 'born-free' among
the internationally-visible Zimbabwean authors, currently living in Scotland) playfully
invites his readers to ponder the compromises involved in the *kukiya-kiya* survival
strategies that Brian Raftopoulos remarks on in this volume. In an era of uneasy political accommodation and hard-to-stomach compromise, philosophy itself becomes yet
another way of 'making do': the township-based family of Huchu's heroine, Vimbai,
has guard dogs called Plato and Aristotle.

The Hairdresser of Harare accurately maps the city of Harare in the period immediately preceding power sharing, both topographically and socially. The novel's action
revolves around Mrs Khumalo's hairdressing salon, situated in the neighbourhood
known as the Avenues: 'Go up from Harare Gardens, skip two roads, take a left, skip
another road and look for the blue house on your right, not the green one, and you're
there.' (Huchu 2010: 2) The salon, in which the novel's protagonist is employed, functions as a social hub and an information-dissemination centre: with prices of basic
commodities rising daily, cemeteries doubling up in size every year, 90% unemployment
and the average life expectancy of 37, employees and customers use this feminised
space to exchange information, tips and advice, and help one another to source basic
commodities and bribe their way to the fronts of various queues. A certain notion of
whiteness still carries social prestige: Sam Levy's Borrowdale Village shopping centre
(swathed in British cultural nostalgia) is still the most desirable place to shop, and
Vimbai sums up her professional attitude by saying: 'Your client should leave the salon
feeling like a white woman.' (Huchu 2010:3) The lives of Zimbabweans inside the
country are represented as always-already influenced by events and processes outside its
borders (as Mufamadi, McGregor and Pasura and Ndlovu-Gathseni variously point
out in this volume): Vimbai's family is for a long time sustained by elder brother
Robert's remittances sent from the UK, and Harare airport is always full of 'black
families who only spoke English in a funny accent – children of the Diaspora.' (Huchu
2010: 188)

Against this backdrop, the novel tells the story of Vimbai, a self-centred, 'traditionally'-minded Pentecostal Christian who is unaware of the contradictions this subject-
position entails. Vimbai is shaken to the core by the realisation that her work-mate,
housemate and would-be lover is a gay man. *The Hairdresser of Harare* confronts a key
area of cultural debate and representation in post/colonial Southern Africa: the problem of forging alternative, non-patriarchal masculinities under social conditions of
extreme violence and lack (on this, see Muchemwa and Muponde 2007 and, more
broadly, Newell 2009). Huchu's is the first internationally-circulating Zimbabwean
novel explicitly to draw the parallel between compulsory heterosexuality, patriarchy
and social violence (of the kind that is, differently, pointed out in this collection by
Alexander and Chitofiri). It does so in part by foregrounding and fictionalising two
contemporary political figures: Solomon and Joice Mujuru, also known as Rex
Nhongo and Teurai Ropa, and described here by Martin Welz and Fay King Chung as
pivotal figures in ZANU-PF's political machinations.

This is not the first time the Mujurus and their marriage have been fictionalised by a
narrative related to the problematic interface between gender, sexuality and national

politics. In 1998, Edmund O. Z. Chipamaunga published a novel entitled *Chains of Freedom*, in which 'Tapi, a woman ex-combatant with a formidable fighting reputation' acts as the guardian of both professional and sexual morality of her husband Gono – also an ex-combatant – whose ambition is to 'become rich and famous by hook or by crook' (Chipamaunga 1998, back cover). I have argued elsewhere that Chipamaunga's novel may be regarded as a fictional forerunner of the twenty-first century Mugabeist national narrative (Primorac 2007). In *The Hairdresser of Harare*, the characters based on the Mujurus may be read as emblems of the deep-running ambivalence that marks both this novel and the present moment in Zimbabwe's cultural and political histories.

Minister M – the formidable former freedom fighter and ruling party stalwart–is a regular customer of Mrs Khumalo's hair salon. She represents the unbending discipline and unquestioning, racially-circumscribed loyalty that officially mark ZANU-PF as a party, and, in particular, a certain kind of ZANU-FP masculinity (on this, in connection with Mujuru, see Christiansen 2007). Always in dresses decorated with images of President Mugabe's face, Minister M embodies the war-like logic that has been theorised as a key component of the African postcolony (Mbembe 2001), and that is also a trait of the Joice Mujuru-based character in *Chains of Freedom*. Dumisani, the gay 'hairdresser of Harare', is in every respect her antithesis. 'Feminised' by his job ('A male hairdresser, who'd ever heard of such a thing!' – Huchu 2010: 7), he is in solidarity with with ZANU-PF's victims, including the dispossessed female white farmer Trina, who supplies hairdressing products to the salon. In Chapter 13, while styling Minister M's hair, Dumisani turns her head wrap into a bandana, and in doing so 'grabbed a pair of scissors and cut it in half, *right through Robert Mugabe's face.'* (Huchu 2010: 59, emphasis added)

But although the novel holds him up as an exemplary figure ('A man so comfortable with his own masculinity was hard to find.' – Huchu 2010: 38), Dumisani's affair with Minister M's husband may, nevertheless, be read as a *ridicule* of Mr M, whom it endows with a status of someone doubly emasculated. This is partly to do with the shape of the plot, which fails to dislodge a certain conventional notion of Zimbabwean femininity – and therefore, the normative national structuring of gendered identities.

Since Dumisani cannot become Vimbai's lover (as she had hoped), his queerness shatters both her personal *and* professional dreams. Her professional standing now cannot be absorbed into his – as it would have been possible in a conventional, heterosexual relationship. And although Vimbai dreams of a perfect male partner, she also (like other modern young women of Harare) desires professional and financial success, which Vimbai's hairdressing skill had initially jeopardised, and then enhanced. Despite the social critique it contains, *The Hairdresser of Harare* imagines such a success as a 'fairytale' opening of as hairdresser's salon at Sam Levy's Village in Borrowdale, financially enabled by Dumisani's wealthy but homophobic family, and authenticated by the patronage of Grace Mugabe herself – the trophy (and 'properly' lady-like) wife of the very man whose face Dumisani has ritualistically destroyed. At the end of the novel, Vimbai keeps her salon, but Dumisani has to leave the country. Minister M has been humiliated, but she has also, in more senses than one, won the day.

If Tendai cannot be Vimbai's sexual partner, he cannot be 'the hairdresser of Harare' either. The price of a happy ending is the absence of radical social change. In one of the novel's last chapters, Vimbai visits a philosophy club run by her brother Fungai, and starts a conversation about homosexuality. As Fungai begins to undo the normative, binary understanding of gendered 'essences' ('between the two genders there are a myriad possibilities' – Huchu 2010:177), other members of the club—despite being outsiders whom everybody else classes as lunatics—get up and leave. In the end, only the mock-Marecheran figure of a friendless youth with a bad breath is left, and the philosophy club collapses forever.

Tendai Huchu's second novel, *An Untimely Love* (available in electronic form only) leaves Zimbabwe behind and addresses the lives of young Asian Britons: online readers have enthusiastically embraced its combination of *Bildungsroman*, romance narrative and revenge thriller (n.a.). Similarly, *The Hairdresser of Harare* enacts its own rejection of firm formal oppositions by refracting textual echoes of both Chipamaunga's popular and Marechera's modernist prose. In contemporary Zimbabwe – as the chapters in this book repeatedly point out – it is becoming increasingly impossible to take sides. It is also becoming increasingly necessary to do what was previously unthinkable. *The Hairdresser of Harare* combines a Pentecostal willingness to cast away the past (on this, see Maxwell 2006) with a subtle reiteration of a nationalist indebtedness to it. The name 'Vimbai' means: have faith. In the context of all-pervading hopelessness, this thought-provoking novel imagines change as a tainted, post-modernist fairytale.

In 2011, Solomon Mujuru died in a mysterious conflagration at his farm-house. In some ways, it was a reality stranger than fiction – not an emasculation, either metaphorically or politically, but many said an assassination. If his liberal critics found him a lowering background figure, his ZANU-PF 'friends' found him deeply uncomfortable. For Solomon Mujuru was one of those in ZANU-PF who wished elections delayed till 2013. He sought time, it was said, for a successor to Robert Mugabe to be found *before* the elections. It was, in Fay Chung's terms, the 'better aspects' of ZANU-PF seeking a fresh way forward, not tied to an old-fashioned nationalistic past but seeking a modern and more flexible nationalistic future. Mujuru had, it was said, encouraged Makoni and spoke regularly to Tsvangirai. But he was, all the same, even with forms of ambivalence hanging about him, a 'hard man', a product of the liberation wars. The 'better aspects' raise the question as to the nature of the 'worse aspects'. In a Zimbabwe of many voices, some conspiratorially silent in public while still seeking change in the corridors of power, the silencing of voice is still an option. But will it take more than the gutting of a large farm-house by fire to silence all the myriad voices who have now found expression in Zimbabwe?

References

Chipamunga, E. O. Z. (1998) *Chains of Freedom*, Harare: Zimbabwe Publishing House
Christiansen, L. B. (2007) Mai. Mujuru: Father of the Nation? In K. Muchemwa and R. Muponde (eds), *Manning the Nation*, Harare: Weaver, pp. 88-101.
Huchu, T. (2010a) *The Hairdresser of Harare*, Auckland Park: Jacana Media.
Huchu, T. (2010b) *An Untimely Love*, Casper, WY: Whiskey Creek Press.
Marechera, D. (1978) *The House of Hunger*, Oxford: Heinemann.
Maxwell, D. (2006) *African Gifts of the Spirit*, Oxford: James Currey.

Mbembe, A. (2001) *On the Postcolony*, Bekreley: University of California Press.

Muchemwa, K and Muponde, R. (Eds) (2007) *Manning the Nation*, Harare: Weaver.

Newell, S. (Ed) (2009) Postcolonial Masculinities, special issue of *Journal of Postcolonial Writing*, 45 (3).

Primorac, R (2007) The Politics of State Terror in Twenty-First Century Zimbabwe, *Interventions* 9 (3), pp. 434-450.

Primorac, R (2010a) The Book Café Goes Global, *The Zimbabwean* 25 February, p. 14.

Primorac, R (2010b) 'Making New Connections': Interview with Brian Chikwava, in J. McGregor and R. Primorac (eds), *Zimbabwe's New Diaspora: Displacement and the Cultural Politics of Survival*, Oxford: Berghahan, pp 255-260.

Shaw, D. (2005) Queer Inclinations and Representations: Dambudzo Marechera and Zimbabwean Literature, in F. Veit-Wild and D. Naguschewski (eds), *Body, Sexuality and Gender: Versions and Subversions in African Literatures 1* (Amsterdam: Rodopi).

Veit-Wild, F and Chennells, A. (1999) *Emerging Perspectives on Dambudzo Marechera*, Trenton, NJ: Africa World Press.

n.a. (2012) *A Book-Licious Story: Interview with Tendai Huchu and Smokey + Giveaway*. http://abookaliciousstory.blogspot.co.uk/2012/01/interview-with-tendai-huchu-and-smokey.html . Web. Accessed 7 May 2012.

Index

Page numbers in *Italics* represent tables.

Ethnic Party Bans in Africa

Edited by Matthijs Bogaards, Matthias Basedau and Christof Hartmann

In Sub-Saharan Africa, the spread of democracy since the 1990s has been accompanied by the proliferation of bans on ethnic political parties. A majority of constitutions in the region explicitly prohibit political parties to organize on the basis of race, ethnicity, religion, region and other socio-cultural attributes. More than a hundred political parties have been dissolved, suspended or denied registration on these grounds.

This book documents the experience with ethnic party bans in Africa, traces its origins, examines its record, and answers the question whether ethnic party bans are an effective and legitimate instrument in the prevention of ethnic conflict.

This book was published as a special issue of *Democratization*.

December 2012: 234x156: 224pp
Hb: 978-0-415-623636
£85 / $140